Other guides for retailers
published by Management Books 2000

The Art of Being Chosen *(Martin Butler)*
Big Ideas for Small Retailers *(John Castell)*
Law for Retailers *(Bill Thomas)*
People Don't Buy What You Sell *(Martin Butler)*
Retail Buying Techniques *(Fiona Elliott & Janet Rider)*
Retail Management *(Peter Fleming)*
Retail Selling *(Peter Fleming)*
The Retailer and the Community *(Peter Fleming & Karen McColl)*

For a complete list of Management Books 2000 titles visit our web-site on http://www.mb2000.com

RETAIL CONFIDENTIAL

Joe Cushnan

2000

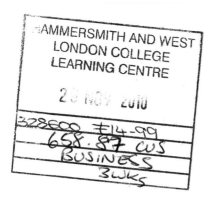
First published in 2010 by Management Books 2000 Ltd
Forge House, Limes Road
Kemble, Cirencester
Gloucestershire, GL7 6AD, UK
Tel: 0044 (0) 1285 771441
Fax: 0044 (0) 1285 771055
Email: info@mb2000.com
Web: www.mb2000.com

British Library Cataloguing in Publication Data is available

ISBN 9781852526474

CONTENTS

ABOUT THE AUTHOR

My career in business management has spanned over 35 years in retailing, wholesaling, tourism, business education, training & development. I have worked in the UK, parts of Europe and the USA for Frank Thomas Group (motorcycle clothing), Asda/Wal-Mart (retail food & non-food), Makro (wholesale food & non-food), The Trustees of the Chatsworth Settlement (Duke of Devonshire – Yorkshire Dales tourism), Alfred Dunhill Ltd (luxury goods), BHS (High Street fashion and home), Young Enterprise (business education) and other business support organisations.

My broadcasting and published portfolio includes BBC Radio Ulster "Saturday Magazine", BBC Radio 4 "You & Yours", The Guardian, Tribune, NZ Management, The Grocer, Retail Week, Edge, Open Eye, Yorkshire Post, The Catholic Herald, Cambridge Evening News, The London Paper, Southern Cross, NZ Freelance, Writer's News, Belfast News Letter, Irelands Own and Fortnight.

And just to keep the creative juices flowing:

Poetry featured in Belfast News Letter, The Cannon's Mouth, Poetry Monthly, Poetic Comment, Bard, Current Accounts, Candelabraum, Decanto, Inclement, Haiku Scotland and Time Haiku.

INTRODUCTION

When I became a retail trainee in the early 1970s, the area manager at the time, a piercing voice wrapped in a Falstaffian torso, came up to me, shook my hand in welcome and said: "Well, at least you're the right height for it." At six feet tall, I did not understand what he meant then and I have no idea whatsoever now. But his comments have stuck with me for nearly forty years as a kind of symbol of the amount of bull droppings there are swilling around in business circles, especially in the war zones of retailing, and particularly in the supermarket sector, a volatile territory more familiar to me than any other. *(Note to readers: I will probably concentrate a great deal on supermarkets but I am confident that any lessons you glean from my recollections and suggestions can be adapted to most retail businesses.)* I have worked then and since with people of all sizes, shapes, genders, races, religions, intellects and classes. Whatever else might be said about retailing, it is a universal activity, a melting pot of a soap opera, but it is also much more besides. The industry is a perpetual motion of cash, people, equipment, stock, time and social influence.

Retailing can be compared to a motorway. Broadly speaking, supermarkets operate in the fast lane, many local stores hold steady in the middle lane and specialist retailers move at a slower pace on the inside lane. It is a busy world with lots of traffic heading for as much market share and customer loyalty as possible. The industry can be your best friend or worst enemy, your Dr Jekyll or Mr Hyde.

There are those who say that retailers, especially big, powerful behemoths, have more faces than Big Ben in their attitudes to employees, customers, fair trading with suppliers, as well as other significant issues such as urban and rural exploitation within a much broader environmental canvass. Supermarkets in particular get the lion's share of boos and hisses as they gain more clout, more land, more of our money and more swagger in the world of commerce. Most times we love them for just being there and other times we hate them when they get too big for their boots, which they have a tendency to do more times than is comfortable.

This book draws on more than thirty years of my life as a retail careerist, with most of my time spent at the sharp end in stores dealing with day-to-day challenges from customers, employees and the unexpected. Mostly, I loved the working environment but I tended to dislike the routines, the interference and the egos. It is supposed to be a simple business but, God knows, many people make it more complicated and frustrating than it should be.

This is not intended to be a comprehensive handbook but I hope from my recollections, opinions and suggestions that it helps stimulate ideas and improvements at best and makes you chuckle from time to time at worst. I hope it is useful for those of you already immersed in your retail careers and a practical introduction for the new, fresh-faced intake that is about to dip its toes into this crazy, challenging but mostly rewarding world. If you do not fall into the previous two categories, then I hope you enjoy it as an entertaining journey as I attempt to illustrate that the retail industry is vibrant, the people are diverse, the management is erratic and the job, rather like a clown's, has traces of despair and elements of fun, requiring a determination to keep pedalling even when the wheels fall off the wobbly bicycle. Enjoy the ride, but please use your knowledge, intellect and passion to improve yourself, your team and your business every day in any way you can.

To set the scene a little more for you and to pander to my fetish for lists, here are two to get us going. I wonder if we both have anything in common here. Better still, make your own lists and use them to enjoy the loves and banish the hates.

10 things I love about business
(What, as many as 10?)

1. Interaction with people (yes, really)
2. Opportunities to hone communication skills
3. Challenge of scaling the heights of customer satisfaction
4. Opportunities to stimulate ideas
5. Challenging team projects
6. Unselfishness from great teamwork
7. Opportunities to develop the skill of humour
8. Competitiveness
9. Pace
10. Cohesion in adversity
11. Celebration of success, including financial rewards

10 things I hate about business
(What, only 10?)

1. Apathetic leadership
2. Poor communication
3. Bad planning
4. Erratic organisation
5. Lousy manners
6. Boring meetings
7. Untidy workspaces
8. Declining morale
9. Mischief-makers
10. Gossips

Most of my retailing experience is UK-based, with odd dabbles here and there in parts of Europe and the USA. To put my analysis, comments, advice and stories into context, it is important to keep reminding ourselves that retailing, with all of its quirks, is a very important part of UK industry. The website of the British Retail Consortium (motto: *For Successful and Responsible Retailing*) lists these facts:

- In 2008 UK retail sales were over £287 billion.
- The retail industry employed over 2.8 million people as at the end of June 2009. This equates to 11% of the total UK workforce.
- 9% of all VAT-registered businesses in the UK are retailers, with the total number currently at 197,990.
- In 2007 there were 297,850 retail outlets in the UK
- More than a third of consumer spending goes through shops.
- Retail sales account for 20% of the UK economy.
- The retail sector generates 8% of the Gross Domestic Product of the UK.
- Sales over the internet account for less than 4% of total retail sales

It is a substantial industry and important in so many ways. But I am glad that it is not perfect, otherwise we would have hardly anything to do and precious little to write about.

P.S. Look out for the "Ssssssssssh! Retail Confidential home truth" alerts at the end of each chapter and bear the points in mind in your ways of working. Retailing is not a perfect industry but it can be ego-driven, pretentious and smug at times. If you are in retailing or thinking about working in retailing, do your best to avoid the negative traits and work to keep strengthening the strengths. Develop a passion to resolve issues raised in your day-to-day work and be yourself, as much as you possibly can.

PART ONE

1

WHO IS THIS GUY?

(special guest stars, Butch Cassidy and the Sundance Kid)

Where better to start a book on retailing than with a reference to westerns. In fact, you may detect when you read on that this is my favourite cinema genre, as I tip my ten-gallon hat to the good, the bad and the ugly sides of business. I am convinced that cowboy movies have influenced my way of thinking during this long management career because of the broad themes of pioneering, challenges against the odds, good guys and good gals, bad guys and bad gals, troubleshooting, the difference between right and wrong, the simplicity of life and the "man's gotta do what a man's gotta do" attitude to finding a way through difficulties. The latter reference, of course, now includes the aforementioned gals because "a gal's gotta do what a gal's gotta do" too. Political correctness may be the last chance saloon where the insane try to buy the sane a shot of whisky, before the fist fight of common sense restores some order. Retailing needs men and women, of course, but much more importantly it needs the best leaders and the best followers to keep developing and growing, regardless of gender. In addition, the odd prickly cactus jabbing at sensitive parts of one's anatomy and the rolling sagebrush blowing past in apathy at a suggestion to one's boss are essential to keep our feet on the ground in the yee-hah, gun-slinging world of retailing. I know I'm overegging this pardner, but, hell, it's a dirty job and somebody's got to do it.

As an avid television viewer throughout my childhood in the 1950s and early 1960s, westerns seemed to dominate the small screen, as well as cartoons. I remember once at school being asked who my heroes and influences were and, instead of choosing someone from history or literature, like Winston Churchill or William Shakespeare, I blurted out: "John Wayne and Fred Flintsone." The class laughed, the teacher looked perplexed, then mortified, and I could not understand what all the fuss was about. I'll leave the Flintsone reference for another time, except to say that he was a man honourable to family values and one of life's triers. But John Wayne and westerns in general helped to shape me as a retailer for the reasons already mentioned. He ran the gamut of all the attributes needed to manage a situation from empathy to ruthlessness, always with true grit. He was not a perfect hero, in fact he was cinema fiction, but there was something about his screen presence and no-nonsense approach to life that seemed to seep into my heart and soul. To see him as Rooster Cogburn in "True Grit" with the reins in his teeth, a rifle in one hand and a pistol in the other, charging the four bandits who were blocking his road, was poetry in motion to a fifteen-year-old. My message in all of this is to not ever deny your roots or influences, no matter how embarrassing your answer to the heroes question. That is my defence in this fragile argument, your honour. Moving on...........

About forty-five minutes into the wonderful "Butch Cassidy and the Sundance Kid", not long after a massive amount of explosives had blown open a safe on a train, sending thousands of dollars floating on the wind, Sundance asks: "Think you used enough dynamite there, Butch?" Before Butch can respond, another train screeches to a halt and a posse of lawmen bound out on horseback to chase Butch, Sundance and the rest of the Hole-in-the-Wall gang. Butch and Sundance veer off in one direction and the rest of the gang ride in another in a bid to split the posse up. But the posse elects to stay together and concentrate their pursuit on Butch and Sundance. After a while, Butch looks back, then ahead to ask Sundance: "Who are those guys?" And it is a variation on that question which may be occupying the thoughts of some people who are considering reading this book. They might be asking: "Who is this guy, and what gives him the licence to write a retail book?" Dear reader, I have had my fair share of rewards and scars from the wild and wacky world of retailing, but I would not change anything – well, except for the odd inept boss or two. My involvement in shops goes back a long way, to a time when JFK was in the White House, Alec Douglas Home was in Downing Street, the Dartford Tunnel opened, the Vietnam war was raging and the first ever Doctor Who episode was shown on BBC television. I make that over forty years ago, and these days you don't get that for major crimes!

I started in retailing when I was nine years old, delivering groceries on a bicycle not dissimilar to David Jason's Granville contraption in "Open All Hours". I am taking you back to the early 1960s and, contrary to what you might be thinking, this was no child labour exploitation. I was employed after school at the Mace supermarket in the Belfast suburb where I lived. I performed several duties apart from deliveries, including shelf stacking, serving on the fresh meat counter, manning (boying?) the till and sweeping up. I loved it and I have no doubt that this experience sowed the seeds of my desire for a retailing career. This was the era of simple retailing, with no frills, no hype, no unnecessary hassles, no price wars and a regular customer flow of loyal punters who came in, did their shopping, had a little chat and left generally happy and untroubled. It was unfussy, straightforward trading.

The reason I remember my age at the Mace is because I can answer that question "Where were you when JFK was assassinated?" On one of my delivery jaunts, I remember very clearly that I overheard a passing pedestrian tell someone else what had happened. I knew it was fairly important news but my mind was preoccupied by the yapping dog behind the railings of a house in Fruithill Park. I was scared stiff and could not pluck up the courage to open the gate. Luckily, after about ten minutes of terror, the woman of the house stepped out, called the dog off and beckoned me up the driveway. I delivered her box of groceries, she gave me a half crown tip – big money in those days, probably not worth estimating the value in today's world of monetary confusion – and I scarpered before the dog was let loose again. Unlike the poor President, I had escaped with my life intact. It is experience like this as well as being a jack-of-all-trades in a shop that can shape a person and even now I draw on those days occasionally to help me think through business problems or advise students on the nuts and bolts of retailing. I still give dogs a wide berth too. It was hard work and fun, a vital combination to maintain interest. It gave me an appreciation of team-working and a clear lesson that getting stuck in was part of the deal. On one occasion, one of the Mace owners told me that if his white shirt was not grubby at the end of his working day, he had not worked hard enough. It was a useful lesson.

After a couple of years in my first real job after school when I worked as an office clerk in the Belfast Corporation Electricity Department, I was so miserable and bored with the mundane work that I started looking for a more exciting, fulfilling and rewarding career. To tell you the truth, the most exciting thing in this office-based job was looking out of the window to watch the monthly capture of stray cats by the "Moggie Squad", as we dubbed them. They would corner and nab the cats with nets and prongs, probably cruel by today's standards but exhilarating to observe. But cat watching did not pay the wages or satisfy an active mind, so I began to look for something else.

Before long, I had entered British Home Stores as a Trainee Manager in Belfast. In the early 1970s, BHS was seen as the slightly poorer relation to the mighty Marks and Spencer, but still a force in its own right in fresh food and clothing. After my nine-months training apprenticeship, I was appointed department manager of menswear as well as being becoming the security coordinator, for these were dark days in Belfast, riddled with terrorist incidents including bomb scares and, worse, occasional explosions. Stores employed security guards at entrances to search customers for incendiary devices and anything else threatening, and it was part of my job to look after this team. It was a pretty ineffective way to stop terrorists but it was the done thing to give customers the impression that we were thinking about their safety. It brought a whole new dimension to customer care and it was an experience that helped me to see the humanity necessary for a successful business life. Tending to customers rigid with shock and bleeding after a bomb exploded outside our shop one afternoon was an extension of customer service that I hope I never have to get involved with again.

But there were lighter moments. In fact, to be coarse for a second, I can honestly say that I have shovelled shit for my employer. On one of the many evacuations we endured following a telephoned bomb scare threat, the police and army contingent brought a sniffer dog to roam the store in a bid to detect explosives. As the brave dog scrambled around and over the top of counter displays, it decided to stop on my department and do its business. After the all-clear, I grabbed a bin and a shovel and scooped the poop before customers were allowed back in. So, whenever anyone talks about rolling up sleeves and getting hands dirty, they are talking to an old campaigner here.

One of our departmental managers' pranks involved a mannequin's hand. Each afternoon, about an hour before the shop closed, our key holder would come in and tour the building to start locking windows and fire doors, ensuring a fully secure shut-down when we all left for the evening. One part of his tour took him down some stairs, around a corner and down a further flight to a fire door at the back of the store. One day, a couple of us disconnected a hand from one of the fashion department's mannequins and placed it on the handrail just around the corner of the stairwell. The key holder, observed in advance by us as a handrail holder as he descended the stairs, almost jumped out of his skin when he touched the cold extremity. He was normally a gentle plodder as he did his rounds, but on that day, he bounded up the stairs and shot out on to the shop floor like a banshee with its tail on fire. In our privacy, we screamed with laughter for ages and he developed a suspicious eye in our company from that day on. It is shameful, of course, in retrospect, but I include it as an illustration that we were prone to a little childish fun from time to time in those days to counteract the seriousness of the business we were in. If we had been identified as the culprits, we reckoned that our defence rested on us arguing that we were only giving him a hand.

I learnt many lessons in the first of my eleven years with the company, especially about the spirit of teamwork and the joys of camaraderie, both of which are not as apparent today as they were then. This was an age of shops opening at nine in the morning and shutting at six o'clock at night, with quite a number closing on Wednesday afternoons. There was none of the modern-day relentless 24/7 pressure and demand and it is probably the "we never close" society that has eroded the closeness and friendliness of retail colleagues in current times. The BHS teams of the 1970s would be in the local pub ten minutes after closing the shops, having fun and, dare I say without sounding too Oprah Winfrey, bonding. We seemed to find common ground and team spirit in our collective fear and dread of our managers who were tough, sometimes uncompromising authoritarians – "old school" status-conscious bullies at times, you might say. The most fearsome of them all, Mr Robinson (for these were the days when we were definitely not on chummy first name terms), would rule his store and his team with an iron fist and a terrifying scowl. He controlled everything and if you crossed or displeased him in any way, you were subjected to the fiercest bollocking you can imagine and you left his presence shaking. He had the sinister knack of arriving on the sales floor and, somehow, exuding an aura of terror amongst the managers. We did not even have to look up. We knew he was there. On the occasions when I did look up, he would be standing a good hundred feet away staring back at me before wagging his come-hither finger. In a terrified Uriah Heep, ever-so-humble way, I would approach him knowing that he had spotted at least three things on my department that needed attention. "Use your eyes, son. Make sure you see these things before I see them." I would nod silently and he would march away to terrify the next department manager.

If you wanted a new duster for your department, you had to take your old one to his office, knock the door, await his barking instruction to enter and then request a replacement cloth. He would be reclining back in his chair, stone faced and, I swear, not blinking. He would grab the old rag dangling from your trembling fingers, hold it up to the light, peer at you through the holes in the fabric and then thrust it back at you. "There's at least half a dozen more cleans in that, boy," he would shout. This was one of my first groundings in cost control, albeit a trifle extreme but a good lesson in watching the pennies. I wasn't rational enough in those days to understand it but when I became a manager myself, I often used this true tale as a benchmark against waste. My team members looked at me with the same quizzical expression I had used a couple of decades before. But no-one can deny the principle of not wasting a business's money unnecessarily.

In another store, the manager decided to change the layout completely. This was a two-floor shop and his plan was to swap the top floor departments for the ones on the ground floor. There weren't many health and safety stipulations at the time and one Sunday, when the store was closed, a bunch of us dismantled, transported and reassembled every counter in the shop, humping fixtures up and down stairs, getting fingers trapped, knees banged, shins damaged and feeling that every nerve and sinew in our bodies had laid themselves down for the good of the business. I recall one of our number renaming BHS as Bangers, Humpers and Screwers, for that is what we were with our hammers, broad backs and do-it-yourself toolboxes. But, despite the hard graft, it was another instance of "we can do it" which we needed in retailing then and continue to need now. It is like a massive hamster wheel and it is crucial that the wheel keeps moving and that we all embrace the need for change and improvement, no matter how scraped our knuckles or bruised our knees become in the process.

The BHS phase of my career took me, as department manager, to stores in Belfast, Manchester, Romford and then Wood Green, East Ham and Hackney in the London area. From the stores, I moved to head office on the Marylebone Road in London to head up a team in a new IT project and then on to the role as UK Audit Manager. By and large, it was one of the most enjoyable and productive periods of my working life and I have a lot to be thankful for to BHS. As a retailer, it taught me about:

- organising time
- routines of morning and evening department inspections
- identifying personal mentors and role models
- a deep respect for people
- the critical nature of teamworking
- the dangers of big-headedness
- how to deal with the unexpected
- a "can do" attitude

- the place for fun in business
- nurturing a genuine love for retailing.

For career development reasons and a decent hike in salary, I left BHS and joined Alfred Dunhill Limited, based near Piccadilly in London, as Administration Manager in the jewellery division. Dunhill, long associated with tobacco, had evolved into a luxury goods empire, mainly supplying fashion and accessories for men. It still had that old-fashioned hierarchical tone to it, so much so that the Chairman at the time, Richard Dunhill, was referred to with affection as Mister Richard. It is easy to scoff at these anachronisms but there is a good lesson in there somewhere about appreciating seniority and understanding that authority requires respect rather than ridicule, the latter being a tabloid and populist pastime nowadays. Yes, there have been terrible business leaders over the years and there have been great ones at all levels in the management structure. There are times in my career when I was great, times when I was average and times when I made some terrible decisions or made no decisions at all. I suspect I am one of a large majority in retailing, trying hard but not always succeeding.

Our department dealt with the worldwide wholesale and retail distribution network supplying watches, lighters, cufflinks and writing instruments – pens to you and me – and other expensive bric-a-brac. The challenge of a position like this was to find the most efficient and effective ways to manage worldwide administration without moving from my London office base. Every now and again a voice from overseas, usually Mr Chung from Hong Kong, would scream down the telephone demanding to know where the gold watches were and what had happened to that special order of cufflinks. This was a very different kind of service with "invisible customers" from various parts of the globe, and in many ways it was a lot tougher than dealing face to face with people. I felt I had to work harder at building trust because, most times, two disembodied voices would be exchanging comments. It was a very good lesson. Face to face or from a distance, customer service and customer care carry the same pressures. I will dwell on service a great deal in later chapters but it is shocking to realise how inconsistent service delivery has been, and still is. I blame myself at times over the years for some of my lapses, but I also hold to account many other managers and employees for failing too. Dunhill was another stretching career role that taught me about another aspect of customer service.

The Alfred Dunhill years improved my skills and knowledge in the following ways. I learned:

- to be more organised
- to work more efficiently from a distance
- to be a more articulate speaker
- to develop a voice with personality
- to understand the need for a trustworthy tone
- to listen actively
- to think on my feet
- to communicate progress frequently
- to follow through on details
- to appreciate the support team around me

One other true story occurs to me about a particular attitude to customers. The Alfred Dunhill Cup, a team golf event held in Scotland, was launched in 1985, supported by one of the sport's most successful players, Nick Faldo. This story has nothing to do with Nick Faldo per se but it does have something to do with photographs of him. One day, as I walked along one of the corridors of Dunhill's London offices, I stuck my head round the door of the guy who was coordinating the event on behalf of the company. We chatted about the exciting launch and he even allowed me to hold the very first Dunhill Cup trophy. On his desk, I noticed a pile of photographs of Nick Faldo and I asked about them. The guy said that he expected quite a few letters from the public requesting signed pictures and he wanted to be ready for the onslaught. I commented that Nick would be busy signing the photographs on top of his other commitments and the guy laughed saying that Nick would not be signing the pictures. "He's far too busy for us to bother him with a job like that. Someone from the office will sign them as Nick Faldo. Who's going to know?" I was flabbergasted and to this day I wonder how many people have treasured signed photographs of Nick Faldo not signed by Nick Faldo but probably by Doris in accounts or Colin in goods inward. Nick Faldo, no doubt, was oblivious to all of this but it stands as an example of how easy it is for businesses to dupe people.

The headhunting call to move from London to the Yorkshire Dales came out of the blue. The Marquis of Hartington, son of the Duke and Duchess of Devonshire, was on the lookout for someone to manage the tourism and retail operations side of his estate at Bolton Abbey, in North Yorkshire. The family pile at Chatsworth in Derbyshire was benefitting from visitors and shoppers and it seemed a reasonable ambition to apply the successful business ingredients to their stunningly attractive Bolton Abbey estate. A friend and colleague from the BHS days had mentioned my name and I agreed to meet Lord Hartington. We met in the bar of the Cavendish Hotel, near Fortnum and Mason in London, and over two halves of lager the tall, angular aristocrat asked basic interview questions before offering me an opportunity to spend a weekend at the Devonshire Arms Hotel at Bolton Abbey as a base to look around the estate and write a brief reflection and review of business improvement possibilities. A few weeks later, after meeting to discuss my report, I was offered the job of managing the various car parks, retail and catering businesses on his estate and to develop a marketing plan to attract more visitors. That was it – no assessment centre, no recruitment palaver, no highfalutin' human resources circus acts of hoops to jump through. Simplicity. To cut a long story out completely about removal vans and jack-the-lads, we moved out of London to the glorious surroundings of the Yorkshire Dales.

As a tourist attraction, Bolton Abbey's landscape is a gift in all its natural and historic glory. On hot weekends and school summer holidays the place was chock-a-block with cars and people, causing the dilemma of welcome tourism income with unwelcome damage to the land from tramping feet, badly parked cars on roadside verges and litter. It was never a comfortable job in that respect. The Estate Manager never seemed at ease with the idea of such a position. He was "old-school", perfectly professional but from a different era and with a different attitude to modern-day commerce and dealing with masses of people. He was more at home with farming, forestry, fishing, shooting and other rural activities. He was not a natural people manager, more the lord, with a small "I", of all he surveyed. His status was almost akin to the aloof Captain Mainwaring, the "Dad's Army" bank manager, with all that blatant superiority in the air any time a lowly serf was in his presence. He was not an unpleasant man, nor a ranter or raver, but we all knew he was in charge. The tenants that ran the businesses dotted around the estate were beholden to the Estate Manager and the landowners and showed little or no enthusiasm for this new retail kid on the block with, in their eyes, fancy opinions on how to run things. I was not arrogant, just different – the runt in their litter, I suppose. The challenge was there, certainly, to develop business, people, service and general operating standards, but the resistance was tangible at times. The job lasted two years before I got the call to go to see his Lordship at the "big house" one Friday morning.

This noble aristocrat who had employed me to develop the visitor attraction on his estate was quite nervous but nonetheless clinical as he explained his decision to terminate the job. The main reason was cost and it affected my "department" which was my secretary and me. The interview was economical, straight to the point, handled with reasonable sensitivity and the support afterwards was fine. The meeting lasted about five minutes. It was quite a shock. I remember leaving the "big house" and driving back to my office to talk to my secretary. We had a cup of coffee, a brief chat and then packed our few meagre belongings before saying goodbye to each other and a few people in the main estate office. Some of our (former) colleagues were very nice about it, showing sympathy, but others remained aloof, perhaps glad that this little adventure had come to an end and they could get back to their "sleepy hollow" existence.

The Bolton Abbey experience was wonderful in many ways. It is by far the most beautiful working environment in which I have ever had the privilege to operate. It introduced me to some genuinely hospitable people and presented me a very different challenge to anything I had ever done before. But, I suppose in retrospect, the main thing I am grateful for is that it toughened me up considerably as I had to learn how to react to and manage a diverse group of individuals from the receptive and naturally supportive to the obstinate and bloody-minded. Unknown to me at the time, I needed that very experience as I re-entered the more mainstream world of business, as a General Manager in cash and carry wholesaling with Makro, and later as a General Manager at Asda. The following chapters, broadly speaking, draw on my combined sixteen years with these two companies and, rather than dwell on too much background detail at this stage, I will refer to various experiences and incidents later. But by way of a brief geographical summary, I worked for Makro in Liverpool, Sheffield and Nottingham, with occasional assignments in the Eccles head office. Following a call from a head-hunter, I worked for Asda in and around Derby, Leicester and Mansfield, with brief periods on projects out of the Leeds head office. They were testing times and golden opportunities to learn more and more about business and people.

But to close off my Yorkshire adventure, here is a list of some valuable lessons from my brief tenure as Tourism and Retail Operations Manager at Bolton Abbey. I learnt:

- to relish challenges out of my comfort zone
- to take time to familiarise myself with individuals
- to hone my presentation skills
- to adapt my body language and voice to individual needs
- to expect, endure and recover quickly from setbacks
- to stick to my professional principles
- to work at displaying a transparent persona
- to understand that not all arguments can be won by me
- to accept constructive criticism
- to enjoy success and learn from failure.

I hope I have illustrated some credentials to explain part of my retailing background and gone some way to answering the question: "Who is this guy?"

Sssssssssh! "Retail Confidential" home truth alert:

I caution myself when explaining my background that personal memory is subjective. I remember a thought-provoking comment from a former mentor that in each of us there are at least three people; the person we think we are, the person other people think we are and the person we really are. Self-appraisal is a good thing but beware glossing yourself up too much. If I have over-glossed, and I hope I have not, disciplinary sandpaper will be applied in due course. As a "home truth" opener, beware, dear reader, of ego and self-importance. Stay as humble as you can. Many retail managers do not.

2

HOW THE SIMPLICITY OF RETAILING CAN BECOME COMPLICATED

Some years ago in an Asda general store managers' meeting, our Regional Director was spouting on about the usual, but important, stuff like improving customer service as well as staff morale. One of our number chanced the question: "But, boss, which is more important, customers or staff?" Without a flicker, rather like the granite features of a black belt assassin, the director replied: "Neither. The most important thing in this business is growing market share." Well that shut my colleague up and threw the rest of us into confusion. After years of "the customer is king" and "people are our most important asset", here we had a new, more modern and much colder take on retailing.

In pure academic terms it is possible, of course, to play the six degrees of separation game between customers, employees and market share because, rather like incestuous communities living in dark forests, they are all connected in one way or another. Market share cannot be achieved without customers parting with their hard earned cash, nor can it grow without effective and efficient company servants to deliver the goods and services.

But let's not get ahead of ourselves. The fundamental financial blood flowing through the veins of retailing is sales. Every sale is an injection of cash into the system and the object of a business's *raison d'être* is to preserve as much of that cash sale as possible in profit. The aim of the whole enterprise is to sell goods that do not come back to customers who do. You may want to re-read that last sentence which, I think, encapsulates the essence of retailing. Think about it. As a retailer you want to sell stuff that reeks of value, quality, reliability and fitness for purpose, as well as complying with all the law enforcement and due diligence shenanigans of course, to happy customers who are so deliriously satisfied that they will not return the goods but will return themselves to shop again and again *ad infinitum* – selling goods that do not come back to customers who do. Once, or ideally well before, the sale has "kerchinged" into the till, the business bean-counters in finance should be looking for ways to glean the most profit from it, after deducting expenditure for wages, marketing, utilities, maintenance and so on. It should not be the retail manager's job to spend disproportionate amounts of time on accountancy matters but unfortunately, these days, administration pressures do tend to curtail the amount of time managers actually devote to active sales and selling, and being visible and available to colleagues and customers. Ask any retail manager worth his or her salt and the majority will tell you that activities and responsibilities off the shop floor sometimes distract them away from the important arena for selling and, especially, for interacting with customers and supporting teams. But the job of this book is not to get bogged down in the frustrations of accounting and administration. We should be concerned first and foremost with our colleagues and customers as conduits to selling and sales. We are retailers, for goodness sake. We should be on the shop floor!

My mention of clowns and their wobbly circus bicycles earlier links to another analogy of retail shop floors, especially big department stores, DIY sheds, hypermarkets and supermarkets. They are indeed circuses full of action, spectacle, display, colour, fun, danger, and lots and lots of people. Customers are the audience and store teams are the performers out to please. Just as the trapeze artist flies through the air from one swing to another and the crowd gasps in wonder, so too must retail staff dazzle and entertain as they buzz around the aisles delighting customers with helpful and friendly service. It might be retailing but it's show business as well, folks, and just as every movie, television show or theatrical play is not perfect, much the same analysis can me made about shops. There are too many poor retailers and not enough exceptional ones, and the diagnosis almost always comes back to service and the people employed to deliver it. Get the people ingredient wrong and retailing suddenly becomes much more complicated and harder work. Get the customer attention wrong and retailing becomes a much more frustrating and negatively emotional business.

During 2007, I kept a diary of customer service to record my shopping experiences – more of that good, bad and ugly stuff later – and it seemed to me that most retailers were not as interested as they intimated (in advertising blurbs and in-store signage) in great customer service delivered consistently by enthusiastic and highly motivated staff – for if they were true to their word, they would take micro-care in the recruitment, assessment, selection and management of their people. Now, I hear retailers retaliating in their droves at this assertion and I know that a great deal of effort goes into job vacancy filling. I have done more than my fair share of assessment centres and interviews for retail positions. I know it's hard work and time-consuming. I know its detailed and a chore. I know that every time we hire an employee, no matter how detailed and meticulous we have been in the process, it is a risk because time will tell if we have made the right choice. But however committed and energetic all of this recruitment activity is, clearly it is not enough.

The majority of my customer service diary experiences from 2007 onwards ranged from borderline average to dire. Like a panhandler, I sifted through the gravel and occasionally discovered a gold nugget, a wondrous example of pure and perfect customer service delivered by someone who enjoyed their job, who wanted to be in retailing and who had either a natural or well-trained gift for it, supplemented by good manners, social etiquette and, darn it, a liking for people.

But most customer service staff (and not just in retailing – I have covered libraries, health centres, taxis, hotels, restaurants, bars, cafés, post offices and so on) were lethargic, disinterested and, in a few cases, rude. Now, let me qualify what I've just said. I have worked in retailing for many years, with many individuals and teams. I understand fully that it can be a very stressful environment. I can recall many people who gave their hearts and souls to jobs they loved, but I also remember some deadbeats and plodders who wanted their wages but chose to do as little as possible to deliver service and add to team morale. Maybe my memory is skewed but it is certainly true in my recent customer research that the deadbeats and plodders are in the ascendancy in customer service roles. Why should this be the case? Why has this aspect of customer service specifically, and retailing generally, become so complicated? Perhaps part of the answer lies in the following true story.

I was in a well-known High Street newsagents and booksellers not so long ago and, as ever in my experience with this particular chain, I saw as I entered that more than half of the tills were closed and a large queue was waiting to be served. I picked up my newspapers, a couple of books and some pens and decided to join the queue which by this time had grown to sixteen deep, with still only half the pay points in operation. When it eventually came to my turn, I asked the girl serving why more tills were not open and she said she thought it was because someone had phoned in sick. But then she suggested that I could speak to the manager if I wanted to complain. I had no intentions of asking for the manager but, as I was invited, I said okay. The manager arrived and I shook his hand. He looked more than a little stressed. I pointed to the tills and the long queue and asked if he thought that what we were witnessing was acceptable customer service. "Believe me, I am not here to give you a hard time because I know how hard this business can be. But, look, what's wrong with that picture?" I was calm and polite because I could see that he was struggling. Nervously, he started to explain the situation, emphasising the sick call from an employee, but then he stopped, paused and looked at me with puppy dog eyes. I could feel a home truth coming on.

"Actually, the real reason is that I don't have enough staff," he said. "My wages budget has been cut by 45% and I have to manage with what I've got." I was stunned by the frankness of his admission. He shrugged his shoulders and looked visibly relieved at having had an opportunity to get something off his chest. I know from my own career experience that when dealing with customer complaints, store managers have to think on their feet and sometimes we make things up to appease people. Sometimes we tell half-truths and sometimes we fib. Sometimes we invent new angles to "company policy" just to get rid of the person we are trying to pacify. We become politicians in a sense and dig deep to find excuses from anywhere in our bank of words, phrases and verbal chicanery. But from time to time, there is nowhere else to turn but to honesty, no matter how painful it is. I looked at the store manager, a little sweat shining on his top lip and I thanked him for his candour. I empathised with him on the basis that I had been in his position many times during my retail management career, pacifying customers, juggling with staff hours, wage budgets, absenteeism and stringent service targets. But I also said that if this example of poor customer service was the norm for his store, then people would go elsewhere for their books and newspapers. He agreed, looked embarrassingly sheepish and apologised. We shook hands and I wished him luck. I reckoned he was going to need it if his costs had been slashed so savagely.

It was not clear from the manager whether the 45% reduction was in hours or cash wages but either way such a severe reduction of people costs carries serious threats to sales, service and morale. It was not uncommon in my years as a retail manager to get a call from head office saying that each store had to save £1,000 on wages that week because sales were tight. As it was a decree, there was no discussion, so out went overtime, absenteeism cover, recruitment and so on. In addition to the orders from above was the emphasis that there was not to be any decline in operating standards or customer service. At times it was very, very tough to manage and, no matter how hard people worked, things began to creak. It all makes cold-hearted business sense, of course, to keep financial matters in order, but it contrasts with the warm words about the value of customers and staff. In this commercial conundrum, cash wins every time. It smacks of the-bottom-line-is-king and tends to diminish the status of the customer. It is the market share ambition pushing everything else down the agenda. It is a simple business doing a superb job of complicating itself.

But let's get back to what makes an excellent retail shop a great place to shop and a great place to work. Remember that retailing is a cocktail of cash, people, equipment, stock and time, all of which have to be managed like the proverbial spinning plates. In short, it's about making things happen, and a lot of the time making things happen against the odds.

I have found over the years that one of the most effective exercises in retailing's fast moving world of frenzy is to stop! I have often mentioned to my teams that if we are always running at high speed through the aisles and across the store, we might see what is ahead of us but everything in our peripheral vision will be blurred. Slowing down, which is criminal to many energetic retailers, is really a good habit to adopt. Go onto the shop floor of any retailer, position yourself anywhere you like, but a fairly central position might be more beneficial, and then stand still. Slowly, very slowly, look around you as far as your neck can stretch and observe the environment. Look up, look down, look ahead, look left and right. Is the shop clean or dirty? Is it tidy or untidy? Is it full or empty? Is the lighting working? Are the staff members busy? Do customers look happy? Are there queues at the tills? There are lots and lots of things to see and, as a retail manager, the ability and confidence to stand still in the middle of a busy shopping area is one of the best ways to spend your time. Why ability? Practice makes perfect and adding to our skills as well as developing the right working habits will always stand us in good stead. Why confidence? As a retail manager, you are being observed all the time. It may be embarrassing to be "caught doing nothing", i.e. standing, seemingly idle on the shop floor. But stick with it. Make notes if you must to prove that you are working. But do it. You'll be amazed at how much you can take in which you can then use when you tour the store to talk to your team about specific actions for improvement. This standing still business is a great way to illustrate retailing simplicity by doing an uncomplicated act, developing a detailed observational eye and asking basic questions.

I remember a bit of anonymous feedback about me on a staff

survey that reported: "Sometimes when I am busy and I look up, he is standing staring into space. It is a bit of a doddle being a manager. Workers do the work and managers are allowed to daydream." Depending on your point of view, feedback can be the breakfast of champions or indigestion for losers. Take the flak, but take the time as well to do the right thing, take time to stand and stare, or more accurately to observe and then act on what you see.

As I mentioned, you will find several lists throughout this book to help you think, plan and act. Here are ten thoughts on how to go about getting things done:

1. Decide if action needs to be taken at all.
2. Once made, don't wrestle with the decision, just get on with it.
3. Always remember, getting things done is what you are paid to do.
4. Better start today than tomorrow, if practical.
5. Aim to complete the task to the best of your ability, heart and soul.
6. Whatever you decide, remember it is your decision, so own it completely.
7. Enjoy the process and learn from the journey.
8. Give yourself a secret personal incentive and strive for it.
9. Think of the benefits to the business, the team and yourself.
10. Involve the whole team, lead but delegate.

There are so many examples of gung-ho retailers who go at everything like a bull at a matador's backside but it really is sensible to take a little time to think things through. Yes, there is a need for instant decision-making and reaction at times, but getting into the habit of calculating the risks, assessing the task and so on can pay dividends when the job has been executed well. The stopping and looking exercise is an act of almost pure simplicity in a complicated, intricate selling environment. But such activity or inactivity is often misconstrued, ridiculed and seen as idleness. It is not and, contrary to all criticism, it should be applauded as a significant, effective management habit. But, if inactivity is seen by some people as management locked in a trance, then the other end of the spectrum, over-excited activity, speed-walking across the shop floor rather like the cartoon road runner, can be just as perplexing to beady-eyed staff. Try walking at speed around a shop and be conscious of your peripheral vision. Clarity is always better than blur. Slow down, if you move too fast. It pays.

Speaking of excitable management and simplicity strangled by complication, I recall this incident. Many years ago, when I was barely out of my trainee manager's nappies, my store manager suddenly decided to empty a forty-foot-long gondola run of wines and spirits because he thought that displaying the booze on bulk pallets would look fantastic, be more accessible to customers and would reduce the amount of time taken to replenish the fixture. On paper, it was the brainchild of a genius but in practice it turned out be the work of a madman. The job was to be done during trading hours, causing frustration and annoyance to customers who wanted to dwell on whether to buy cheeky Claret or randy Rioja. Without any consultation, the manager barked instructions for us to start emptying the shelves and dismantling the fixtures. We worked so hard that even our sweat was sweating. Once we had cleared the space where the wine gondola had been, we observed the manager whose face had taken on the distorted look of a gold-medal-winning Olympic worrier. We glanced, uncomfortably, at each other and then back to him. For a while we were like the nodding heads at a Wimbledon final. Eventually, he gathered us round and said: "You know, this isn't going to work." "We know," said one of the team. "Well why didn't you speak up, then?" He seemed to be engulfed in a crimson mist, a mixture of anger and embarrassment, perhaps. I think we all gasped in unison but we had little choice other than reassembling the fixture, putting everything back the way it was. It was a classic scenario involving the guilty party blaming everyone else around him, and all this Laurel-and-Hardy fine mess nonsense could have been avoided with a little thought, team consideration, customer awareness and some adherence to the ten points above. The laws of simplicity should have prevailed but the jaws of complexity had clenched around the boss's cerebral cortex.

Thankfully, there are fewer and fewer clumsy managers around these days, as far as I am aware, and most major companies tend to keep strict central control of layouts and space management anyway. I realise that in businesses with small shops, more licence may be given to managers to experiment with merchandising and display. If the manager in the wine gondola case had given the team an opportunity to get involved and if he had attempted to listen to ideas and opinions, maybe things would have been less soul-destroying and disastrous, less complex and more simplistic and sensible. The ability to listen is an essential skill and here are some tips to help you:

- Fix your concentration completely on the person speaking.
- Listen calmly and professionally.
- Listen as they talk but leave your analysis and judgement until later.
- Learn to take notes in your head.
- Keep your body language open and welcoming.
- Avoid closed questions when probing for more understanding.
- Allow the speaker plenty of time to finish what they are saying.
- Interrupt only if you have something relevant to say.
- Guide them towards the crux of the matter.
- Be prepared for mixed emotions.

Planning and listening can also be linked to motivation. Every team leader and business manager has a responsibility to get the best from the team. No-one can afford to fly solo in retailing. It is a team game. Once at a training session I was running, a young manager raised the point that she preferred to work alone because she was sure the job would be done correctly if she did it herself. The group then embarked on a discussion of the point she was making and a consensus developed that it was not possible for a manager to work in isolation especially in a retail environment. Eventually it was the young manager versus the rest of the managers in the room. In a last-ditch attempt to win the debate, the manager cited her example that Paula Radcliffe had won marathons and broken records on her own, so therefore it was possible for people to achieve great things by working solo. But as soon as she had finished explaining her example, the manager was rounded on by others in the room who responded by saying, yes, Paula Radcliffe was indeed the key athlete but behind her was a team of coaches, trainers, physiotherapists, nutritionists, agents, public relations people and so on – a team game! The young manager agreed to disagree, but secretly I think she agreed but liked a robust debate. I have worked with managers puffed up by their inflated egos and senses of their own importance. Some of these selfish mavericks really believed that they were supreme in the decision-making process and that no matter what anyone else thought, they would always come in with what they insisted was the one and only right decision. Occasionally, I have witnessed eggs on faces and finger-pointing when plans have turned sour. Let me repeat that retailing has never been, is not and will never be a one-person affair. Teams make things happen and here are some tips regarding team involvement:

- Involve, involve, involve everybody.
- Be available for anyone, anytime.
- Give individuals wide but clear parameters to do more than their job.
- Praise successes however minor.
- Coach people out of failures by identifying opportunities.
- Encourage fun, laughter and team socialising.
- Talk to each member of your direct team at least once a day.
- Keep everyone informed about the state of the business, warts and all.
- Encourage ambitions to do well.
- Ensure you as leader are seen to be doing your job well.

Do you remember how my old boss banged on about market share? Well, market share, if indeed that is the most import business goal, comprises many things, including, nay *especially*, people. Individuals and their talents are extremely important, but it is as a collective force that things get done, things like the efficient management of cash, people, equipment, stock and time.

As I have been banging on, retailing is supposed to be a simple selling and service business but in looking for easier and easier ways to trade, the industry does tend to get caught up in complexity, occasionally unnecessarily so. Sometimes, external forces like changing legislation, due diligence procedures and acts of God impose complications, but mostly, internal erratic management decision-making and superfluous interference add to the burden. I'll try to navigate through some more of the complexity in the next few chapters, including specifically a look at workplace culture. To prepare for this next part of our journey, I would like you to sit comfortably and read a modern fairy tale.

Sssssssssh! "Retail Confidential" home truth alert:

Retail businesses are motivated by growing market share primarily, with customers and employees acting as mere pawns in the process. Individuals are not as important as they think they are. Retailers pretend that retailing is a simple business, over-complicated for many self-inflicted and external reasons – but the guiltiest of the guilty parties that make it complex are, eh, retailers themselves!

3

HOW RETAILING CULTURE CAN BECOME CONTAMINATED BY SNAKE OIL

Once upon a time there was a business called ZZZZ. It sold goods and services to millions of customers. ZZZZ was big, powerful, influential and successful. It had a defined culture. It had a mission statement. It had ten values. And it employed heroes it was proud of and probably some irritating villains that had slipped through the recruitment net, although anything negative about ZZZZ was not admitted openly. The ZZZZ culture was simple:

"We will honour our individual commitment to be enthusiastic company representatives by loving, encouraging, supporting and serving our customers, our colleagues, our guests and all our other stakeholders. We will do this with a 24/7 positive attitude, with personal honesty and integrity and by total loyalty to the ZZZZ brand. We pledge to see no ZZZZ evil, speak no ZZZZ evil and hear no ZZZZ evil."

The ZZZZ mission statement was clear:

"To be everything and anything our customers want us to be. We spend all our waking hours in a ZZZZ state."

The ZZZZ values were strict commandments:

1. We are the company in heart, mind, body and soul, human and spiritual investments in ZZZZ.
2. We worship the sacred name of ZZZZ.
3. We behave like every day is a ZZZZ day, in work and out of it.
4. We honour the history and purpose of ZZZZ.
5. We shall not waste ZZZZ time, ZZZZ money or ZZZZ opportunities.

6. We will be good ZZZZ neighbours to those living and working around us.
7. We will show ZZZZ respect to all people, all beliefs and all races.
8. We uphold the truth, the ZZZZ truth and nothing but the ZZZZ truth.
9. We will treasure the purity and spiritual satisfaction of being a ZZZZ representative and ambassador.
10. We will be loyal to ZZZZ until our last employed and living second, until our last breath.

ZZZZ, believing its own spin, thought of itself as the perfect company with the perfect culture, perfect directors with perfect employees selling perfect ranges with perfect service. Of course, it was not perfect. It could never be perfect. Could it?

The problem with a lot of businesses is the ease with which they are suckered in to the latest snake oil platitudes dressed up as academic literature. In the context of this book and maybe lots of others, the term "snake oil" refers to bogus medicinal compounds originally sold by dubious carpetbaggers in the United States when the west was being won. The "oil", or however else panaceas are dressed up and expressed, may seem like a remedy but it could well disappoint the believers, and most times at the height of snake oiliness, disappointment was and is rife. It is much the same today with cosmetics, for example. Just listen to the amount of invented scientific claptrap that appears in advertisements. It is a contest between facts and sham, and aspects of company cultures fall into much the same traps, worlds where fantasy grapples with reality.

But, I digress slightly. The ZZZZ fairy tale, if packaged into a slim volume and tagged with some kind of professorial blurb extolling the virtues of the magic potion recipe within, might sell millions of copies *(Note to self: What the heck are you writing this stuff for? There's gold in all that guff!)* making business leaders believe that they had found a new, radical and invigorating way to run their companies. Now there's nothing wrong with education and intellectual challenge, but if these guru-hungry executives would put the books down and get off their posteriors, they would gain much, much more information and ideas if they spent a disproportionate amount of their time working with their teams at the sharp end.

I am reminded of the chief executive of a company who had read a new and exciting book of ideas for best practice and greater efficiency, and decided to ban e-mails and all other written communication in his business on Mondays and Fridays in a bid to force human communications by encouraging people to walk from desk to desk, office to office, colleague to colleague. He felt that meeting people in person or conversing on the telephone was a good thing, and no-one could really argue with that. But he soon found out that the biggest drawback was that his teams stored up their banned e-mails throughout Friday and Monday and come Tuesday morning unleashed an avalanche of e-mails, memos and bulletins, thereby negating any real advantage to his gimmicky initiative. He believed the theory of the book but failed to turn the notional idea into a practical improvement. Not long into the experiment the idea, like all the copies of the book he had bought and distributed, were cast into a corporate skip.

Business books are all very well – in fact, a few of them are excellent, albeit only a few – but sometimes they can be too academic and therefore as dull as a politician's memoirs or scary as an undertaker's diary, whilst others can be too shallow, slight and prone to unqualified pretensions. At best, books in both categories can contain some inspirational ideas but at worst they encourage modish meddling and a tendency to fix what ain't broke. (By the way, I realise I am treading dangerous waters here for critics of this work, but, hey, what's life without the odd risk?) The one major advantage with slim (less than 100 pages) books is that you can browse them easily and quickly in bookshops without having to buy them. (If you cock your ear and listen carefully, you will hear publishers whimpering.)

Many business books are aimed at executives who are keen, or desperate, to come up with something different to help improve their businesses. There is nothing wrong with an intention like that. But there may be a tendency for some executives to want to look and sound intelligent just by carrying a book around with them. I recall in the 1980s that the writings of Tom Peters, the brash and dynamic modern guru, took hold of many management types and buzzwords and phrases began to litter the corporate landscape like never before. Peters, in his heyday, was a trailblazer but hundreds of other writers have jumped on the book wagon since in search of a fast buck, driven by money ambitions rather than the noble cause of business and people development. At least that's how I see it, because I spent a fortune on lots and lots of these books in the 1980s and 1990s, and, at the risk of sounding like my Granny, I would have been better off putting the cash into my Post Office savings account. In the course of writing this book, I looked through my business book collection and noticed now what I failed to realise then, that most of the writing was self-congratulatory drivel at worst and platitudes at best, with an occasional rose among the literary thorns. There are many I do not trust any more, but I still enjoy and revere the straightforward work of people like Robert Heller, Charles Handy, Dale Carnegie, selected bits of Tom Peters and, of the more modern books, Allan Leighton's "On Leadership" where he draws a lot of good sense from his high-powered friends and colleagues in business.

So, there is nothing wrong with using books and other supporting material to stimulate ideas in theory but in practice if the whole thing becomes a flash-in-the-pan burst of activity that is allowed to die away after a few months, the exercise becomes expensive to the balance sheet, confusing for the employees and potentially detrimental to the integrity of the executives who could be seen as trend followers rather than trendsetters. Sometimes the book titles can be warnings in themselves to encourage caution rather than hasty acceptance of their doctrines. In my experience, retail companies over the past decade or more have embarked on cultural change crusades influenced by US management thinking, by and large. But, not pointing accusatory fingers at any book or author, here are ten business book titles to inspire or scare you:

- *Sack Your Boss* by Jonathan Jay
- *The Happiness Paradox* by Ziyad Marar
- *Our Iceberg Is Melting* by John Kotter and Holger Rathgeber

- *My Boss Is A Bastard* by Richard Maun
- *The Energy Bus* by Jon Gordon
- *Who Moved My Cheese* by Spencer Johnson (read this one Caerphilly!)
- *Get Weird* by John Putzier
- *I'm Not Anti-Business, I'm Anti-Idiot* by Scott Adams
- *Inside The Tornado* by Geoffrey A Moore
- *The Empty Raincoat* by Charles Handy

Of course, I realise a certain irony in all of this by writing a book called "Retail Confidential" and I will let others be the judge of my quotients of inspiration or scariness. If you browse the pages of Internet booksellers or bookshop shelves, you will see vast amounts of available material to help cure all business ailments and we should all be encouraged to fish around for the books that appeal to our needs for solutions or learning. However, like a fisherman, we should be very selective about what we bag for later consumption and what we throw back into the river.

I have not read all of the books in the list above but I am trying to illustrate that business and business gurus tug us in different directions as we attempt to analyse, criticise, understand and advise our way through life. My advice based on experience is to enthuse people to read and learn, and to keep reading and learning, but also to be selective in the messages and lessons we draw from books and other training material. The substance is not all good, it is not all correct, it is not all relevant and it is not a cure for all business ills. We should be more and more alert and tuned into what is good, correct and relevant, and what has a higher than average chance of at least some success. One book, like one size, does not fit all, so beware – where there is intelligence and depth, there also may be bluster and shallowness. The ZZZZ fable is a warning that perfection, i.e. consistent perfection and success, is as elusive as the second bestselling album from many long-forgotten X Factor singers.

The development and management of harmonious workplace cultures are things to be encouraged and I suppose if something good comes out of a book to move the process a step further to Nirvana, then that is okay up to a point. In my Asda career, the company chant –

"Gimme an A, gimme an S, gimme a D, gimme an A" – was another aspect of tribalism, made in America, that made many of us in the UK feel uncomfortable. Sometimes the management team in stores would chant this rap in unison in a back office and other times, with perplexed customers looking on in a mixed state of amusement and horror, we would perform it on the sales floor. I have lost count of the number of times I have stood with the rest of my colleagues hand-clapping our way through this ritual nonsense, pretending that a company song, chant, promise or oath of allegiance to enthuse us for the day ahead was something worth doing. This may still be routine tribal ceremony in many businesses across the world. It is embarrassing and awkward for most of the participants and, dare I say, sometimes it has the opposite of the intended effect because it deflates rather than inflates spirits. But companies that believe in the ra-ra, start your engines, let's get ready to rumble school of employee excitement tend to frown upon anyone not contributing with visible relish and passion. However, occasionally, something weird can happen and the urge to nip off and hug a customer becomes strangely compelling. So, rather like ghosts and ghouls, aliens and close encounters, there may be something in it, but, again, let the employee beware.

The encouragement of an all-inclusive business culture was once a fad but now it has become a trend, essential it would seem in commercial industry if one's venture or enterprise is to be taken seriously. The danger is that people can forget that retailing in particular, and business in general, is essentially straightforward. It is the people that make it complicated. Here are some broad business definitions to help keep our feet on the ground. Business can be described as:

- buying and selling stuff
- a commercial activity as a means of supporting livelihoods and economic growth
- a process of selling things that do not come back to customers who do
- a commercial enterprise, profession or trade operated for the purpose of earning profit
- a commercial activity demanded by customers

- a legally established entity designed to provide goods and/or services to consumers
- the purchase and sale of goods and/or services to maintain investment opportunities
- the activity of providing goods and/or services involving financial, commercial, industrial and social ingredients
- simply the process of supplying demand in an economy
- a money-go-round of managing valuable assets.

I recall spending most of a training day debating the definitive wording for a business's purpose and, of the twenty-five people in the room, we came up with more than a dozen definitions, miles away from the one we were desperate to find. The truth is that business can be many things to many people and it is a useful exercise for all of us to take a few minutes, once in a while, to attempt our own up-to-date definition. It can help to maintain or refresh focus.

Regardless of any precise wording, there are urges every now and then for businesses to veer off the track and catch the bus to "Whimsville", when looking for the next big cultural change. A few years ago a middle manager at a company I worked for dashed rather enthusiastically to the chief executive's office and waxed lyrical about a visionary book he had read on a holiday beach. This book, one of hundreds of similar slim volumes churned out by rather slow-drawling American business consultants, purported to guarantee that its 180 pages were filled with a new doctrine to motivate people in any organisation. It was called "Gung Ho!" and it drew its messages from supposed Native American beliefs in the wonders of nature. The three big themes were encompassed in the spirit of the squirrel, the way of the beaver and the gift of the goose. No, honestly, I am telling the truth, cross my heart and hope to give you the context of our interpretation of this respected work. There we were, United Kingdom citizens (and here in this international brotherhood you can insert your own identity, for you too, international brothers and sisters, are vulnerable to this stuff) with more in common with cats, dogs, budgies and hamsters, about to spend a three-day training course in the beach resort of

Blackpool being gung-hoed. My dictionary defines the term "gung-ho" as unswervingly dedicated, loyal, and foolishly enthusiastic. Staring through the biting sea winds of the north west coast of England, we wondered if our American cousins far across the Atlantic would believe that a bunch of Limeys had fallen for this management pantomime stuff. Our venue had been prepared to resemble a forest with wood shavings on the floor, cardboard trees and cushions pretending to be tree stump seats. We would learn that the spirit of squirrels in their industrious search for nuts fulfils God's plan for the forest. The way of the beaver in their organisational ability to build dams fulfils God's plan for beavers generally and the gift of the goose is God's gift that we give ourselves because, I suppose, geese in their honking, cheery way, encourage each other along, especially on winter flights. Our job on the course was to discuss and analyse all of this natural education and interpret it into a practical philosophy to help develop business, customer service and people. One of my colleagues remarked to me that it was all uncomfortably tribal and Waco, referring to a disastrous American religious cult incident, or possibly whacko. Whatever we thought, our collective body language, learned from another course, was expected to be very positive. The directors had adopted a kind of spiritual air to demonstrate that it was possible, even for them, to be saintly in hard-line business.

Mission and values marketing is now seen to be important for a company's public image, but even more pertinent for employees to devote themselves completely to their employer and their work. In a nutshell, where the Bible teaches us to love God and our neighbour, corporate leaders have taken and extended the idea to urge employees to love customers, love each other and believe in the company's essential contribution to society, a kind of parallel to the ZZZZ scenario. In my long retailing career, I can remember the exact wording of my employers' mission statements and values as clearly as I can remember my religious education questions and answers, my prayers and almost all of the text of specific church services. Why these commercial strap-lines are ingrained in my mind is not so much a mystery when I recall that we were encouraged, if not forced, to recite the words verbatim every day until we convinced ourselves and our superiors that we were a loyal, faithful workforce. There was, and is, a tendency to develop workplace cultures drawn from quasi-religious foundations. If an employer can harness the vocal chords of hundreds of thousands of employees daily to proclaim the wonders of the business, then power and influence become hypnotic partners, affecting individual beliefs. It is a chemistry that church leaders might consider studying and adapting, perhaps.

But we have enough to do to understand how business works without delving into the catacombs of religion. In addition, pouring snake oil on top of complexity may be a badly worded summary, but hopefully you get what I mean. It is from off-the-wall training and culture-changing activities that the language of business can become contaminated with incomprehensible words and phrases. In the spirit of jargon, let us run a few up the flagpole and see who salutes or throw a few words into the ideas wok and give them a darn good stir – whatever we do most of what follows in this list is useless, but you might just hear stuff like this in your organisation. You have a duty to kill this claptrap stone dead by refusing to allow stuff like this to escape from your lips.

- *Holistic integrated synergy*
- *Strategic team-based opportunity*
- *Virtual group-wide solution*
- *Total enterprise scenario*
- *Radical focused paradigm*
- *Pro-active relational compromise*
- *Harmonisation extension campaign*
- *Digital culture engineering*
- *Heads-up interpersonal mining*
- *Deep-dive coal-face restructuring*
- *Optimum cerebral energy*
- *Considered spontaneous planning*
- *Incremental offshoot spreadsheet*
- *Data slice and dice*
- *Lights-on inspiration off-load*

- *Critical cornerstone dynamics*
- *Executive narcissism wipe-out*
- *Chill-out defrag time slot*
- *Robust recognition initiative*
- *Ballpark leverage solution*

It all sounds as if it just might be intelligent preaching but it is really snake oil pseudo-intelligence – just flush it away!

I know I may be sounding very cynical about this modern, catchy, trendy way of enthusing company teams and building happy, productive workplaces, but I can also see that these buzzword bonanzas can be enormous fun, and fun counts. When I worked for Asda, our annual conferences were a mixture of condescending but probably necessary prattle, the odd important theme and a good old dollop of fun. Here is a list of some of the stuff we were given to remind us about key messages as we returned to our stores:

- A plastic hot cross bun that we were ordered to take to the bakery each day as a quality control check. Any real buns that failed to match the prototype were to be binned.
- A coat hanger to remind us that we were a "no jackets required" business (a kind of "no status" thing) and to get our sleeves rolled up to work with our teams.
- A small plastic bin that we were encouraged to carry around the supermarket as we picked up litter, renegade grapes and magazine junk mail inserts, a symbol to everyone to keep the store tidy.
- A ten-foot ruler, again to carry around the store, as a measure to think about the importance of greeting staff, customers and whoever else came within our ten-foot orbit.
- A tape measure, endorsed with instructions, to ensure we maintained "customer space" between fixtures and a reminder to control the heights of displays.
- A slab of rock (although to be fair, this was delivered, as it was solid, about four feet high and as heavy as a slab of Yorkshire stone can be) which was placed outside stores declaring the company's value message.

- Rolls of stickers saying "Cut the Crap" which we were to attach to unnecessary paperwork and return to the sender in head office.
- A lot of baseball caps over the years with the message of the moment of the front.
- An instruction to train everyone in the store's fresh food departments to sing or hum the song "Happy Birthday" every time they washed their hands as it was reckoned that the song lasted the necessary length of time to achieve satisfactory hygiene.
- Tons of folders and presentation packages that would make a rain forest wince, most of which ended up in drawers or on shelves untouched, unused and in no danger of being bothered.

In addition to my opinions and illustrations of company cultures, some do get it right, or as right as possible. In my personal experience, having worked for five years at Asda and then five more years when it became Asda within the so-called Wal-Mart family, I could see and sense that many of the values were driven with a degree of sincerity, although it has to be said that the delivery and execution of these values was very inconsistent from board room to shop floor. The original and continuing Wal-Mart values as defined by the company's founder Sam Walton are as follows:

- Commit to your business.
- Share profits with employees.
- Motivate your team.
- Communicate everything possible with your team.
- Appreciate your team's efforts.
- Celebrate success.
- Listen to everyone in your business.
- Exceed customers' expectations.
- Control costs.
- Swim upstream... do things differently from competitors.

The values which are still very relevant today, over forty years from conception, have been condensed into three handy phrases to remind Wal-Mart and Asda employees, or associates and colleagues as they are called respectively, of a more condensed set of ideals:

- Respect for the individual
- Service to our customers
- Strive for excellence.

Before Wal-Mart acquired Asda in the late 1990s, the UK supermarket adopted the values below, eventually simplifying them to the current Wal-Mart three above:

- We are all colleagues, one team.
- Selling is a universal responsibility.
- What we sell is better value.
- Through selling we make our service legendary.
- We hate waste of any kind.
- We must improve the business every day in every way.

Tesco treads much the same solid ground with words and phrases to frame its stance on culture and commitment:

- Understand customers.
- Be first to meet their needs.
- Act responsibly for our communities.
- Treat people as we like to be treated.
- Work as a team.
- Trust and respect each other.
- Listen, support and say thank you.
- Share knowledge and experience.
  ...so we can enjoy our work.

In retailing, these models of values are as good as they get. So, I suppose I am saying here that slick books, conferences, words and phrases have their uses but my advice is to take most of it with a pinch of salt, because it is how these values are implemented, nurtured and managed that counts. They need to be practical and workable or they will just become yawning platitudes. Remember, the gold prospector standing knee-deep in the river will find more worthless pebbles than gold nuggets in his pan, but he perseveres because he knows that amongst the dross, there is the hope of finding something worth getting wet for. If that is not enough to ponder, let me try to elaborate some thoughts on customer service and then lighten the mood with a few true stories in a bid to prove the customer is always......fickle, to say the least.

Sssssssssh! "Retail Confidential" home truth alert:

Company cultures are driven sometimes by whims and fantasies rather than by the needs and wants of the people who work there. Executive egos and business gurus can be detrimental to the enterprise and its human resources, and trying to sound too intellectual in business can make us all look like fools. The best mantra by far from the past three decades is "Keep it Simple" and the best advice is to be a healthy sceptic, although many retailers continue to believe the unbelievable. ("Snake oil salesman on the phone, Mister Grimsdale." "Tell him I'm too busy dealing with reality.")

4

HOW THE CUSTOMER IS NOT ALWAYS RIGHT BUT IS ALWAYS ESSENTIAL AND SOMETIMES SURPRISING

It can be a mantra or a manacle, depending on your particular point of view, bestowed on every one of us by Cesar Ritz, the legendary Swiss hotelier. He puffed out the words, "Le client n'a jamais tort," which translates as "the customer is never wrong," or as we all like to chant it out nowadays, "the customer is always right." Each phrase in its own way is highly debatable because the customer is not always right – but certainly, however you cut it, the customer is always essential. And if the customer is to be elevated to a position of regal importance in the commercial world, then customer service staff should be given parity in the corporate structure. Excuse me, but I thought I heard a voice in the distance shout: "Are you out of your mind?"

Checkout assistants, information desk staff, call centre operatives, banking personnel, catering teams, hotel receptionists, bus drivers and so on are all on the front line in business, facing or communicating with masses of customers on a daily basis. They are trained, hopefully, in personality, professionalism, etiquette and charm, to maintain eye contact, generate warmth, offer huge dollops of sincerity, friendliness and helpfulness, all to make the complete service package fresh and unique to every individual customer. In other words, they carry an enormous responsibility as business ambassadors and hold considerable power to win loyalty through satisfaction or customer desertion through apathy or carelessness.

It is challenging work that does not suit everybody. Some service employees are naturally gregarious but others, through glum facial expressions and lazy body language, display their blatant wishes to be somewhere else, well away from customers and the passing general public. Service needs dedication, loyalty and, yes, significant financial reward. While directors spend some time with customers and lecture on service and goodwill from the relative safety of boardrooms, hourly paid staff put up with the human race with all its foibles, emotions, tantrums, demands and expectations. The experience can range from the sublime to the vile. Serving the public is a tougher and tougher vocation that deserves the best customer servants that money can buy.

Retailing generally and supermarkets specifically are as good hotbed examples of customer service inconsistencies as any. In these arenas, there are more first-hand experiences among service employees of anger, insult, abuse, snobbery, lies, deceit and bullying than there is politeness, friendliness, reasonableness, decency and respect. It is becoming the norm to be a dissatisfied, frustrated complainant and, as a result, front-line service teams have become easy targets. The tendency for all of us to accept the grumpy old man and grumpy old woman personas for personal gain or amusement is potentially dangerous to society and unhelpful in business circles. I know because I have been a part of the nasty side of retailing in supermarkets, superstores and hypermarkets for a long, long time. In fact, Sir David Attenborough could do a wildlife series based around supermarket checkouts across the country to highlight some of the feral behaviour of customers, and occasionally but to a lesser extent, the attitudes of service staff. It is a potential flashpoint in retailing, human being versus human being. Thank goodness most transactions are calm and reasonably efficient, but the chances of a bust-up in the course of a day's trading are very high.

One of the reasons why service employees are easy targets is partly due to their employers raising customer expectations ever higher to levels impossible to deliver consistently. Frontline retail teams bear the brunt, carry the scars and deal with the stress for unrealistic remuneration. Customer service employee wages are, in the main, far too low. If service is to be a major platform in the battle for retail survival and power – er, market share – more investment in payroll and carefully selected people will be essential. If you pay peanuts…. well, you know the rest.

As retailing and other businesses evolve, customer service staff will become a more and more critical and precious resource, entitled to be paid and given incentives in direct correlation to the amount of time they actually spend in the company of customers. If, say, a supermarket checkout operator spends 95% of his or her time with customers, there should be an honest reflection in their rate of pay to acknowledge the supreme importance of their work compared to, say, a director who may spend about 20% of their time at the coalface. Now, to avoid senior executives choking on their Danish pastries, that is not to say necessarily that directors should be low earners but there should be a customer service ingredient within pay calculations to reflect its true importance. If the customer is always right, is always king, queen and precious to the business, service support employees should be handpicked carefully and not subjected to the lottery of assessment centres and inconsistent interviewing standards. We would not rush our purchase of a gold watch or a new house because we know that the decisions are important for our lifestyle. So why do companies risk reputations so often when it comes to recruiting precious employees. Low rates of pay tend to attract candidates of mixed ability and attitude. The pace of retailing puts pressure on managers to put backsides on seats without unnecessary delay.

Many, many mistakes are made and one only has to spend a day at a shopping centre, on a city High Street or in a supermarket to prove that UK retail service is inconsistent, verging more towards average, sometimes appalling, than excellent. The key to major improvement is more thorough recruitment scrutiny and much, much higher wages. But retailers seem determined to pay as little hard cash as possible, blurring the debate by flaunting packages of benefits to inflate the value of remuneration. Some of these benefits include 20% off at the dry cleaners or a free entry to a theme park or four car tyres for the price of three indicating, perhaps, that a benefit is only a benefit if it is actually beneficial to the recipient. If financial cash flow is critical to a business, then business leaders must understand in parallel that financial cash flow is also critical to employees.

At this point, I offer you a choice: either you can break away from this argument and gaze out of the window for a flying pig, or you can give due and serious consideration to the reality of retailing, hospitality and other service providers now and in the future. The truth hurts and, sometimes, so it should. The cries of derision about the impact of wage costs on businesses to get even close to my suggestions are predictable. Remember I mentioned earlier the poor manager who had nearly half of his wages budget taken away from him. If that kind of example is not an indication of cash first and customer second, third or last then I don't know what is. I have spent more than thirty years in businesses trying to control wages and salaries and I understand the difficulties with this kind of maverick opinion. But the blunt facts are undeniable.

The deliverance of customer service on a daily basis is not a pleasure, generally speaking. It is a chore, a grinding, frustrating chore and it deserves proper reflection by bosses who seem more inclined to devote their time to other things. Yes, directors pontificate at corporate conferences about the value of people and their appreciation of their teams, rather like political spin to make the right noises to key audiences, but if they continue to fail to put up the payroll money to support their supposed sincerity, customer service will remain as inconsistent, or possibly get even worse, than now.

Companies swell with pride at the millions, nay billions of pounds of profit but play down or try to clumsily justify the low wages of important staff. Other aspects of business are reinvented or revolutionised, mainly via state of the art, sexy technology or in some cultural regeneration like the ZZZZ example, so why not customer service, or more specifically the proper appreciation of customer servants? The idea is more of a dare than a challenge and where are the business leaders brave enough to take it on?

Now, I did promise you a couple of true customer stories to illustrate that whilst companies have to wrestle with their consciences, customers retain the ability to surprise.

I swear to you that this is a true story, albeit embellished for entertainment value. It happened in my presence and it illustrates that even after three decades of dealing with customers, there is always one to surprise you. Here goes.

One day, in the phase of my career when I was a hypermarket general manager in the Midlands, I took a call from a Mrs Parker (name changed to protect the insane).

"I'm really upset," she began, positioning herself on the front foot and me on the defensive back foot.

"Oh, I'm sorry. Please tell me about it and I'll do everything I can to put things right."

"I don't know where to begin," she replied with a slight choke in her voice and, I envisioned, a tremble on the lower lip.

"Why not start at the beginning? It's a very good place to start," I suggested without the slightest hint of sarcasm, even though Julie Andrews was singing the do-re-mi song in the back of my head.

"Well, I do all the catering at home for my husband's business clients. We have dinners and he discusses things with them while I play host, do all the cooking and ensure everyone has a great time, and, of course, hopefully help my husband to agree some deals."

"I see," I said, silently slurping up the milk skin from the top of my coffee.

"Last week," she continued, "I spent a lot of time working out the menu and I decided to start the meal with avocado pears, prawns and a light vinaigrette dressing. So, as usual for my supplies I came to your store to do my shopping. I picked up two avocado pears, did the rest of my shopping and went home. The next day, the day of the business dinner, I prepared the avocadoes and on cutting the two of them open I noticed they were not pure green. They were mottled brown. I was horrified, with two hours to go until my husband arrived with his clients. What was I to do? The whole evening was about to be ruined. My husband always insisted on three courses, starter, main and dessert and then on to coffee, brandy and cigars. But I had no starter. It was catastrophic. I could feel my blood pressure rising. I could feel my nerves begin to jangle. I was in pieces."

"I'm so sorry to hear this," I breezed in, thinking quietly that Mrs Parker could have opened a tin of soup. "So how did the evening go?" I ventured, realising that as soon as I asked, I risked the wrath of an answer similar to that experienced by a dark humorist who enquired of Mrs Abraham Lincoln: "Apart from that, First Lady, did you enjoy the play?"

"How did you think it went?" blasted sparky Mrs Parker. "It was a bloody disaster. My confidence in the kitchen and as a dinner party host is shattered. What are you going to do about it?"

"Well," I began, not really knowing how to proceed and looking around the office for any object that would inspire me to resolve this tricky complaint. I saw the stapler but, instead of screaming out a message of hope and reconciliation, all it did was encourage a thought in my mental airspace to consider ramming my hand down the telephone to clamp Mrs Parker's lips together. It seemed a great idea, but like most great ideas, impossible without much more time, money, research and determination.

"Well, first of all I am very sorry to hear about your troubled evening. It is certainly never our intention here to upset customers. I know from what you told me that the avocado pears looked perfectly fine from the outside, although I appreciate your disappointment when you opened them up. Perhaps you can help me. What would you like me to do for you?"

I would like to take a moment to give you a short history lesson, in the interests of context, about the avocado and attempt to illustrate how this inanimate object can ruin a supermarket manager's day. For the record, the avocado pear, also known as the alligator pear, was introduced to the USA in the 19th century in Fallbrook, California. It is a town of approximately 29,000 citizens and calls itself the avocado capital of the world. It hosts an annual avocado festival every spring when the good folks of the planet Avocado presumably descend for a feast fit for a Martian. The pears come from trees that grow to about 65 feet and each tree yields 120 pears per year. Each pear can be anything from 7cm to 20cm long and weigh between 100g and 1000g. The pears are relatively cheap to produce and to buy, which is why I shudder at the thought of how

I resolved Mrs. Parker's complaint.

"I have calculated that each dinner party costs £75 and I will be happy if you compensate me that amount for the disaster." Mrs Parker sounded aggressive and committed to her tactics. I wondered, fleetingly, if she ever considered running a political party or a training school for nightclub bouncers.

"Oh," I reacted, sounding faintly like an Alan Carr impersonator, "that's a lot of money for a couple of pears."

"It's not about a couple of pears," she erupted, with backing vocals and harmonies from her band mates Etna and Vesuvius, " it's about my confidence, my blood pressure, my husband's business, my marriage, my, my, my trust in humanity."

To cut this long story short, Mrs Parker and I agreed on the £75 and I filed away a lesson for life, that a couple of insignificant, crinkly green fruits can have so much impact on a life. It worked out at £37.50 per pear and pro rata there's a Katie Price joke in there somewhere. It's the small things that can make the biggest difference. On the plus side, I had saved two loving souls from destroying each other and their livelihood, I had won back the trust of a disgruntled customer and I had developed an aversion to avocado pears for the rest of my life. In the career chariot of commercialism, sometimes a wonky trolley wheel can send you sideways and even though your heart is telling you to empathise and sympathise with people's troubles, your head is urging you to advise them, politely of course, to go away. In the words of the American consumer crusader Ralph Nader: "You're best teacher is your last mistake." Whatever you or I think of this story, the avocado customer is still a customer. The management frustrations (mine) are still frustrations. It's all part of business, it all matters and, even with crinkly green produce, it can all be resolved. In the next chapter I will relate in light-hearted fashion some more true stories that happened on my watch, to debunk the myth that the customer is always right.

On the subject of customer service generally, the following is an account of what really goes on behind the scenes in retailing, what retail staff truly thinks about customers and how insincere retailing can be behind the seemingly friendly mask. Every large organisation is likely to have a customer care department, the conduit through which complaints and compliments can be channelled to the relevant people and departments throughout the business. Such a department is the human equivalent of a computer firewall, preventing the customer (virus?) from getting through to the wrong person and causing almighty chaos – picture the scene if young Giles in accounts payable picks up the phone one day and is confronted by (gasp) a customer's voice! In addition, centralised call centres have sprung up and spread like wildfire throughout the world in a bid to control, formalise and structure customer feedback, and also as a tactic to keep customers several hurdles away from actually speaking to the relevant person.

On the surface the plan is to deliver efficient, polite, friendly and helpful service to customers and streamline procedures, script responses and explanations and so on to help businesses to do just that. It can all be a bit clinical and sanitised, but perhaps it is the best way for a conglomerate to manage this aspect of communication. I spent a couple of days observing a customer care department in a large retail company as part of my induction into the business. The atmosphere was calm and professional, as I monitored various operators dealing with a range of calls from customers. Occasionally I could sense an operator listening to an angry caller, but her placid and polite manner was a credit to observe.

Away from the telephones, at lunch, by the coffee machine or chatting in the corridor, a number of operators let their professionalism slip with negative, sometimes abusive and rude comments about customers including jibes about race, accents, stammers and general demeaning criticisms and jokes. It was all a far cry from the scripted performances in the customer care office environment. It reminded me of political spin, using words and phrases in a carefully contrived presentation package to sell an idea, whilst in the background hardly anybody believed a word that was being said – in other words, all gloss and little comparative substance or sincerity.

The operators, off the job as it were, complained that most customers were out for as much as they could get. It was no longer enough to offer an apology alone and have that accepted. Of course, the apology was an important first step, but many customers demanded recompense in some way, mainly cash or gift vouchers before they declared themselves satisfied. I must say I was a little shocked at the juxtaposition of professional customer servants, polite when doing the job but scathing when away from their posts. It's an integrity issue. Maybe it doesn't matter if customers do not hear the coarse and insulting remarks, but within an organisation, if customers are the main priority for business growth and success, then a more genuine and sincere team of employees should be delivering consistently great service and believing it wholeheartedly on the job and off it. The cynical service staff may be in the minority, but as long as they exist they risk dragging customer service standards down to unacceptable levels and they insult the genuine service crusaders working hard to be professional and polite always, even when communicating with customers that rant, cheat, lie and have predetermined motives when calling.

I remember dealing with a customer complaint that ended in the most peculiar demand. A man came to see me one Friday afternoon and explained that on eating a slice of a baguette, he discovered a piece of metal that looked like a stud from an earring. He emphasised the danger of this foreign body in the bread and pondered that it could have choked him or a member of his family to death. When he mentioned death, his face froze in the fashion of a Halloween mask, just in case I did not understand the gravity of his complaint. I apologised for the problem and asked him if I could have the remainder of the baguette and the metal stud, assuring him that I would send it to the customer care team in head office. Reluctantly, he agreed. I told him that within a few days, we would get back to him with an explanation.

On the following Monday morning, I received a telephone call from the man who explained that he had a letter from head office apologising for the baguette problem. The letter writer was unsure about how the metal stud had managed to find its way into the bread but she did offer the man £20 in gift vouchers to emphasise the company's apology. The man told me that he was deeply insulted by this offer of £20. I ventured to ask him: "What would you consider a reasonable amount to be?" He retorted: "At least £50 and……..(a long pause for dramatic effect)……..a set of garden furniture." The silence hung like a stallion's undercarriage for what seemed like minutes. I spluttered that I could agree to the £50 but as to the garden furniture, he would have to get back to the customer care letter writer at head office. He seemed happy enough with this arrangement and I thanked him for his call. After taking a breath, I telephoned the service person that had written the letter to advise her of the situation and pleaded with her not to give in to any request for garden furniture or anything else from this opportunist. She agreed, and the punch line to this true episode is that more than ten years later we have yet to hear from this man again. The worrying thing is that in another company with another manager and another customer care assistant, another complaining person could walk away with an apology, gift vouchers and a set of garden furniture because canny customers know that some of us retailers are hard and stubborn whilst others are soft and cowering. Such is the inconsistency of business, business policies, management resolve, staff responsibility and customers' intentions.

So if you really are an ambassador for your company, with all the professionalism and etiquette that it entails, then look at how you think about customers on and off the job, observe how your colleagues behave when discussing customers and clamp down hard on any derogatory remarks before the disease spreads. Centralised customer care departments are all very well but they all rely on individuals who do just that – care!

I coordinated a useful training discussion session to test the water on this important subject. I ask the assembled audience to break into groups of three and challenged them to come up with all the words they have used about customers or they have heard within the business without resorting to the word "right". The challenge was for them to complete the phrase: "The customer is always……"

The ensuing discussion depended on total honesty, but if done properly this type of debate can lift the lid of lots of customer service issues and help to eliminate quite a few negative vibes. The following list illustrates some of the responses to the statement during that training session:

The customer is always.....

- .....*important*
- .....*choosy*
- .....*getting on my back*
- .....*nice*
- .....*interested*
- .....*in a bad mood*
- .....*great*
- .....*impatient*
- .....*first, no matter what we're doing*
- .....*after something for nothing*
- .....*a pain in the neck*
- .....*surprising.*

The session was lively and diverse. I brought it to a close by saying that I agreed with everything that had been said because the people saying these things were on the front line, face to face with customers every working day. I also concluded by stating that it is preposterous to suggest that the customer is always right but it is critical for business success, now and ongoing, that we truly believe that the customer is always essential.

Here's a list to help and remind you about the importance of customers.

- Remember customers are flesh and blood like you.
- Consult with them frequently to understand their needs.
- Be crystal clear as to what you do and what you guarantee.
- Think about transactions as steps in building positive relationships.
- Never lie and never over-promise.
- Always return telephone calls and answer mail promptly.

- Answer customers' questions clearly and honestly – you are in business not politics.
- Apologise when necessary and exceed expectations to make things right.
- Surprise your customers' with little rewards throughout the year.
- Ensure your team's commitment to the highest standards of care, on and off the job.

To round off this chapter, I came across a 2009 Chelsea Building Society survey on values and how they have changed in the past twenty years. The respondents, in the 18 to 24 age group, cited the importance of companies that take the time to assist, service with a smile, people giving up their seats for the elderly, pregnant and disabled, respectful children with good manners and saying please and thank you. Now, there's a manifesto for a better world.

Sssssssssh! "Retail Confidential" home truth alert:

The customer is not always right and there is a great deal of hypocrisy in how customers are viewed by service individuals and teams, as well as leaders and managers. Some customer care people could not care less and some company service policies are not worth the paper they are written on because they are not implemented and practiced with sincerity. Some managers fail to lead by example. Much more worrying is the fact that some companies do everything in their power to pay their customer servants the lowest possible wages and risk hacking customers off through inconsistent delivery. In addition, some customers disgrace themselves by exploiting the system and cheating their way to compensation.

5

HOW A CUSTOMER DIARY EXPOSES THE GOOD, THE BAD AND THE UGLY STATE OF SERVICE AND WARNS US TO BEWARE OF "LEMON-SUCKERS"

I know I sound a little obsessive about retailing but, as I mentioned earlier, for a few months I kept a diary of the customer service I experienced in my normal, everyday life because I was becoming very frustrated at what I felt were declining standards. The intention was that the diary would offer evidence, one way or the other, to prove I was right or to exonerate the retailers I was criticising. I approached the research with an open mind, promising myself that I would record my experiences fairly and accurately, and with a sense of humour. I think the diary content illustrates both a problem and a challenge, namely how to achieve high levels of consistency in customer service and care.

As I planned the diary, it occurred to me that in my career as a general manager with wide experience of developing businesses, customer service and people, I have crossed paths with some of the most successful commercial leaders in the United Kingdom. Several of these executives are "graduates" of Asda/Wal-Mart and are among the most successful and influential people in customer-driven businesses today. I met them personally via business visits, office appointments, training courses, conferences and regular group meetings. In their own, unique ways, each one of them is a template for effective leadership. I should emphasise that in my career I would neither consider myself a high-flyer or a low-life and I certainly did not occupy the same ethereal orbit as they did, but I observed them as a footsoldier observes generals, occasionally was inspired by them, sometimes frustrated by them but always fascinated to see if they could deliver the changes and improvements they so often preached to us. The one common bond they have is a firm belief in the continuous improvement of customer service, hence their special guest starring appearances here.

Allan Leighton, committed pluralist, after his phenomenal success in Asda/Wal-Mart and involvement in enterprises such as Royal Mail, BHS and Sky television, is a giant of business innovation and more often than not triumphant against the odds. He recruited me for what turned out to be a ten-year career with Asda. I remember being interviewed by him in a room decorated with beach balls and a huge inflated banana. There was a great emphasis in those days on serious cultural change having a large element of whacky fun. His outgoing personality and ongoing enthusiasm as well as his ability for the common touch brought much needed energy, focus and improved morale to the company. He was practical in his approach, repetitive in his evangelistic recital of the company's purpose, mission and values, and the best example I can think of as an ideal business team leader. He taught me a number of things, including the need to decide crystal clear business direction, commit to the agreed strategy and then stick to your guns to see the job through. Leighton rode commercial shotgun to Archie Norman in the big Asda turnaround in the early 1990s. He is a genuine business hero of mine and, as mentioned earlier, his book "On Leadership" is one of the best I have ever read because it contains real pearls of wisdom from some of the best industrial minds around.

Archie Norman, a wise man in business and politics, once invited me to meet him at Asda head office to talk about the company and how I could contribute to its progress. We had tea and, regardless of my initial ten-minute slot in his diary, discussed my CV credentials, skills and achievements, and his vision, for an hour and a half. His total focus on the job overpowered any desire to engage in small talk. His personality was more controlled than Allan Leighton's but their chalk-and-cheese differences somehow fused together to make the most effective duo in any business at the time. His chemistry with Allan Leighton was a potent and effective cocktail. Norman dipped his toe into political waters as a Member of Parliament and as a senior figure in the Conservative party, but left that world and returned to business where his reputation is stronger than ever. Observing and listening to him, he taught me to spend time on strategy and to put as much energy as needed into spreading the word and convincing colleagues over time through words, actions and example that it was possible for all colleagues to believe in the "one team" philosophy and in their collective ability to change a business for the better. His passion for and personal involvement in the ideas and suggestion scheme gave Asda a people powered boost on the road to renewal and recovery.

Richard Baker, former CEO of Boots, was involved in an Asda senior management development course with me and displayed a penchant for business and a natural charisma and etiquette for leadership. His record of achievement in marketing, trading and turning vision into reality is remarkable. At conferences on stage and in person, he was always warm, intelligent, approachable and interested and that is precisely what he taught me about management with personality, presence and good manners.

Justin King, CEO of Sainsbury's and doing an excellent job, once upset me by auditing an Asda hypermarket that I managed. He surveyed the store to assess various operating standards and gave me mostly positive feedback, along with a few actions to improve. In his final written report, circulated a couple of days later to key directors and senior managers in the company, the balance of the report had tipped completely in a more critical direction. Instead of the mostly positive comments to me in our face-to-face meeting, the latest report contained almost all negative comments. So, my trust in him was damaged and I had a few reasons not to like his style but, with the passing of time, I am a great admirer of his retail success. He honed his skills by growing the Marks & Spencer food business, before resuscitating Sainsbury's, his finest hour to date. He taught me, by default, to be straight with people. But whatever the pros and cons of these superb, passionate and driven business leaders in my experience, it cannot be denied that they were – and probably still are – customer champions, but even these supremos have failed to crack the problem of inconsistent customer service delivery. If the best of the best have problems and challenges, there is still much work to be done for all the rest of us lesser mortals.

The following extracts from my customer diary pick up the subject of inconsistency through real examples of good, bad and ugly service, and offer these leaders and others across industry more evidence to understand the causes of service lapses and, more importantly, opportunities to identify actions for improvement. Throughout the diary, I refer to "lemon-suckers". These are customer service employees who have returned to work straight from the world lemon-sucking championships still sour-faced, concave-cheeked, purse-lipped and squint-eyed from the acid intake, which has now turned, seemingly, to bile. In short, lemon-suckers look as if they despise the human race. Now, whilst this is a retail-driven book, there are instances of customer service from other industries in the diary. I think it all helps to reflect on the state of service generally. As a sort of disclaimer, I have not been specific about particular branches or locations as I do not think it is relevant within my intended context. My point is to offer some real thoughts and observations, not to identify individual locations or people.

DAY 1

It is New Year's Day. I could kid myself and say that this was my limbering up day to get ready for this customer service diary, but I would be lying. The thing about lying to oneself is that one is on a hiding to nothing. This was a chill-out day to contemplate the old year, to reflect on the new year and to convince myself about things that I know already – that pints of bitter, glasses of red wine and champagne, thumping disco music and several rounds of the hokey-cokey from the night before have a negative effect on the bodily constitution the following morning. Still between naps and bad movies, I managed to formulate my customer service plan for the coming year. Like the previous night's shenanigans, it's a dirty job but somebody has to do it.

I tell my family about my customer diary project and they look at me agog.

"Why are you doing that?"

"I want to understand more about customer service."

"Why?"

"It is important."

"Is it?"

"Well, yes, because we are all customers and we should be served better."

"And a diary will help this how?"

"Erm, by collecting evidence of good and bad service, of course."

"And this will make a difference how?"

"Well, it can be used to help companies to improve, you know, in training sessions."

"Do you seriously think anyone will be bothered by the scribblings of a nutter?"

"Ah ha! Insults apart, that is my point exactly. This diary could become my sole purpose in life to warn future generations and visiting aliens of the perils of being a customer."

"Well, aren't we a bloody ray of sunshine on New Year's Day?"

"Happy New Year everyone." I sigh and slump back in the armchair to snooze my way through "The Great Escape". But I remain determined to make this diary relevant.

DAY 2

In this commercial world of retail food standards and other things, the red, amber, green coding method seems to be taking over. This traffic light approach basically means that red is bad, amber is okay and green is very, very good. So, I muse, if red is bad, why is it Tesco's dominant corporate colour. If amber or orange is okay, is that good enough as Sainsbury's choice and is it a genius move for Asda to have chosen the very positive colour green?

SAINSBURY'S: The biggest problem with my local Sainsbury's is its erratic approach to checkout cover. In an aside from a fellow queue buddy, the idea of every customer donating their Nectar points back to Sainsbury's to help them afford more checkout operators seemed to have some merit. I know that the days after Christmas and New Year are slow and dull but customer service people need to perform like pantomime characters. They need to be up for it, to put on a show even if they don't feel like it. Oh yes they do! I encountered my first lemon-sucker of the year who looked as bad as I felt. I had asked him where I could find black pepper. He looked at me as if he was studying a fossil in Time Team. He had obviously not finished his personality transplant post-operation treatment. Eventually he pointed the way, not even bothering to accompany me to the correct aisle. Silently, I recalled the famous W C Fields line: "Start every day with a smile and get it over with." A few yards later I asked another staff member and she was helpful enough to take me directly to the pepper. We exchanged New Year greetings and off she skipped. Same company, same recruitment scrutiny, same induction, same training – different outcomes. What is that all about?

DAY 3

MICHAEL'S HAIRDRESSING: Michael is an old-fashioned businessman, not in any insulting sense, but more in his manners and easy conversational banter with his customers. He is a one-man band and is always ready with a warm welcome, entertaining stories and controversial opinions as he cuts and, very importantly, finishes off the whole process with an equally warm and appreciative parting comment. It is the kind of small-town, individual approach to customer service that huge corporations try to replicate, but, unfortunately, to levels of inconsistency which boggle the imagination. How hard is it for every customer service employee to be warm, friendly and polite every time? The answer it would seem is very hard! Michael has this amusing sign on his wall: "Why is it that all the people who know how to run the country are driving taxis and cutting hair?" I think I could add to that sentiment the notion that he could teach business a thing or two about basic service etiquette delivered in a natural style. Put simply, it is part of him, a natural way with people and a strong believer in please, thank you, have a great day and see you soon plain old good manners.

DENTIST: To a lot of people, the choice between going to the dentist or gouging your eye out with a spoon would have the majority reaching for the cutlery drawer. But these things have to be done unless you want to drink liquids for the rest of your life. In the past, my recollection of dentists' receptionists, rather like those of doctors', is of automatons programmed to give out clipped information with the minimum personality. But today was a revelation. The welcome was cheery and the brief banter was jolly. The waiting room was clouded in the usual misery though, not helped by the television broadcasting one of those angst-ridden morning chat shows. Still, I must not grumble too much. I still put dentists in the same category as garage mechanics. In much the same way, it is too risky to disagree or argue with them. Either way, it ends up costing you money because they have superior expertise in their own fields, or at least a menacing set of pliers. Perhaps the solution is to have all my teeth pulled out and to stop driving!

DAY 4

WH SMITH & COSTA COFFEE: Peckish for a blueberry muffin and a small Americana, I chanced upon this coffee shop tucked at the rear of WH Smith. To get to the café, one has to pass through the shop. The first thing on display is a queue of eleven people waiting to be served at a bank of nine tills, with only five of them open for business. It seems to be a given in any WH Smith of my experience that queuing is acceptable and part of the company's policy, and shoppers should accept and lump it. They have even built controlling walkways full of impulse merchandise to tempt waiting customers. WH Smith would defend itself and declare its undying resolve to create the best customer experience but then the theory of policy gives way to the reality of queues. What a blessed relief then that I was not ready to buy my newspapers. The Costa Coffee shop beckoned. I know why they chose that name. Have you seen the costa coffee in these places? Ha, ha! The young man serving was an excellent example of professionalism, efficiency and care. His friendly approach and good eye contact made the beverage and bun taste all the sweeter. I swear even my wallet smiled. His personality and demeanour seemed effortless and he was very impressive overall. Later, satiated and happy, I selected my newspapers and I went to the WH Smith tills and, lo and behold, the queue had disappeared and I had a free choice of which till to approach. The girl on the checkout was pleasant enough but there was no eye contact, very little conversation and the weakest of parting comments. Unlike the human face of the coffee man, this was a robotic performance from someone who was ambivalent to the very reason she was standing in a customer service environment.

DAY 5

POST OFFICE: This small Post Office is tucked away on the edge of town. It has two service windows, both manned on this occasion. At my window, the lady serving was very polite and helpful. I noticed the man serving at the other window was more of a grunter and a heavy-sigher, and miserly with his warmth and personality, not given to exchange any merry banter whatsoever with his customer. He was not quite a lemon-sucker, but only because he did break into the faintest of smiles once – either genuine humanity attempting to escape, or maybe gastric wind. I imagined him saying to himself as each customer approached his window: "Thank you for not annoying me any more than you already do." It was a benefit of the doubt moment.

WH SMITH: This is one of the most annoying companies in my experience for poor customer service. I cannot recall going into any branch of WH Smith in the UK and feeling that I had had great service. I have been in branches with seven or eight till points and only two manned to tend to queues of twelve or more. Today, in this small shop, of the two tills at the front only one was open and a queue of eight had formed. Another assistant was shuffling some paperwork next to the closed till and, astonishingly, the shop manager was standing less than two feet away. He was either oblivious to the spectacle before him or he chose to ignore this appalling example of dire customer care. This was an incredible example of not leading from the front and of treating customers like cattle. I lasered my eyes into the back of his neck and thought: "Well, aren't you a waste of two billion years of evolution."

SAVERS: From the frustrating WH Smith's experience, I crossed the road to Savers to buy a few toiletries. Here, there were four till points, only one open, a queue of five and another assistant doing some administration work. As I had time to observe, this administration assistant walked over to the person on the open till and chatted away, looking up occasionally at the queue before dropping his line of sight to the counter top. As customers, we felt like intruders. Both of these Savers employees have been admitted to the lemon-suckers club. In addition, one of them was also a gum-chewer. You could almost hear their inner-selves saying: "We're not anti-social, we just don't like people."

HEALTH CENTRE: Obviously, the policy here is to employ only fully qualified lemon-suckers. On my asking for a repeat prescription, the assistant, missing only a nose wart, a broomstick and a cat with evil green eyes, barked some clipped questions and told me to come back in a couple of days. If civility was taxed, she'd have been entitled to a full refund. I hoped she didn't trip on her miserable chin on the way home, but it would have been quite funny if she did. I left, knowing my place in the National Health Service.

DAY 6

I laughed at Max Davidson writing in the Daily Telegraph. He was describing the French art form of the contemptuous gesture and came up with the Londoners' retaliation repertoire of expressiveness. I likened a lot of it to the worst kind of customer service staff – the shrug, the raised eyebrow, the quivering lip, the "whatever" expression, the double tea-pot handle (hands on hips stance), the cold nod, the limp-wristed wave and the Prescott, which is a behind the back V-sign to insult someone without them knowing about it – sadly all true, but priceless. A cynic might grumble: "I can only please one person each day and today is not your day, and tomorrow isn't looking good either."

DAY 7

Today, I reflected on customer service in the light of scant responses from directors to my letters regarding a business consultancy proposal. A director is generally regarded as a person who sets the example, leads from the front and encourages consistency of commercial performance, operational standards, and customer service throughout the organisation. In fact, many directors preach wonderful corporate sermons about the importance of customers, the regal status of clients and the continuing ambition to grow the business. I seem to recall Charles Dunstone of the Carphone Warehouse saying that everyone is a customer or a potential customer and therefore each time he receives communication from a member of the public, he tries very hard to reply professionally and specifically to the person. It is a small but not insignificant etiquette policy designed to ensure that the boss is adding practical and polite action to the continuous positive image campaign for the good of the business. Everyone would agree that this approach makes perfect sense. It is an investment in possible future business from new customers as well as a protection for existing clientele. It is also good manners.

But, not all directors have this attitude and instinct. By default, I performed a survey of key directors in nearly 200 companies, some of them in the FTSE and others in different parts of the private sector. I had an idea that I wanted to pitch to and discuss with company leaders. I had not set out intentionally to survey the response rates to my proposal from directors, but I was horrified to summarise that less than 6% of directors had taken the trouble to reply. Now, I realise that I do not have any right to expect replies, but I was astonished that I was not even being considered as a potential customer by many of these businesses.

On a basic level, the lack of response was just plain rudeness. On a commercial level, it opens up the serious question of whether or not the 94% of directors who did not get back to me care enough about their businesses, their corporate and personal images, their customers and the future. How many of these non-communicative directors have stood up at conferences or written memoranda about customer service standards? How many of them have chastised or disciplined subordinates for failing to deliver professional customer service? How many of them have signed their names to customer charters for their employees to follow in the daily routines of business life? How many of these non-communicative directors would recognise hypocrisy if they looked in the mirror? I write this diary entry from two points of view. One is with disappointment that communication standards have fallen so dramatically over recent years, especially amongst our industrial and commercial leaders who should not only know but also do better in their treatment of that thing we call the general public. My second platform is one of passion. I have worked in and around retail for over 30 years and I know how difficult it is to respond to every telephone call, letter, email and face-to-face comment. I admit openly that I was not and am not perfect in this regard, but I have the Dunstone ethic to try extremely hard to respond to all communication within a couple of days. If directors do not have the same mannerly passion, then they are probably hurting themselves and their businesses without even realising it.

In addition, being involved in business education, delivering enterprise programmes to audiences of college students, I regret, but will not shy away from, having to use factual anecdotal evidence from real company life to illustrate some of the subject matter. Students often think of directors as supposedly perfect employees, who can be expected to display high standards of personal presentation, professional and, yes, good manners when dealing with employees and customers. Directors must be the best in their businesses, otherwise they would not have reached the heady heights of the boardroom. When I smash the myth of good etiquette, students are as disappointed as I am. However, it is a note of encouragement to these students, some of whom will become business leaders no doubt, to ensure that they return good manners to corporate life when their time comes.

To the 94% of silent directors, I worry about you and your businesses. There is probably not an old saying on this but there should be along these lines: "As you slide down the banister of corporate life, may each pointed splinter in the seat of your pants be a reminder of all the instances of lousy communication with your customers." To the 6% who responded, I congratulate you on keeping the flame alive with your polished manners and fine sense of customer importance.

DAY 8

SAINSBURY'S: Sainsbury's have their snappy little Jamie Oliver-endorsed slogan "Try Something New Today" but I wish they would try some old tricks like opening enough checkouts to avoid queuing. They have a checkout for baskets only and an adjacent checkout for 10 items or less. Most times they open one or the other but not always both. So if you have a basket with 11 items in it, you invariably have to join a queue of trolley-pushers. The controllers of the checkouts walk around with Madonna mouth-microphones looking important but not always in control of the situation. Maybe I will fill in a feedback form and suggest a suitable orifice for the mikes. But, easy as it is to criticise, I always try to bring my opinionated self back to earth by recalling this comical advice: "Before you criticise someone, you should walk a mile in their shoes. That way, you will be a mile away from them and you will have their shoes."

DAY 9

B&Q: In the name of all that is holy, as my mother would say, why can't shops like this open more checkouts when they see queues forming? What makes it worse in B&Q and other DIY stores is that you can be standing there with a bag of nails while the guy in front has a trolley laden with planks, bags of cement and other stuff that takes ages to process. What made it even more infuriating today was the sight of three B&Q staff talking away on the service desk, oblivious to the customer frustration building to their left. I swear the planks had more get up and go than them.

DAY 10

On the radio and in the newspapers, there is talk of the January blues brought on by miserable weather, mounting debts, failed New Year resolutions and broken relationships. They say that the blues will stretch to the end of March. Oh Lord, how many customer service staff will be affected – a lemon-sucker with an added dose of the blues doesn't bear thinking about. There was a survey in a magazine on how to be happy and keep smiling. It was a kind of a multi-point plan: relationships – keep your relationship productive (eh?); mind – a happy brain makes a happy person (only if it and you gets 8 hours sleep each night); body – eat 5 portions of fruit and vegetables a day (go easy on the prunes) and exercise regularly; stillness – relax and meditate, (but not while you are on the checkouts on a Friday night); emotional intelligence – know your emotions and how they affect others (this has nothing to do with some of the customer service robots in shopping centres); live in the present – take part in activities that involve a sense of flow (eh, again?); the environment – make sure your body has at least one hour of broad daylight every day (but that might be a problem for some of the Gothy vampires in service environments and some nightshift workers); technology – avoid excessive technology (turn your mobile phone off, mate); challenge yourself – confront your fears and limitations (nothing that a good employee appraisal wouldn't expose, methinks); take control – live deliberately, not accidentally. There is enough substance in this kind of psychology to help improve some aspects of human behaviour and the human condition. But too much psycho-baloney can just add more complications to simple human business transactions. The trouble is that more and more people read, believe and adopt this kind of thinking without batting an eyelid. It becomes convenient to adopt new revelations and new dogmas to counteract the stresses and traumas of modern living. *Note to self: remember to throw a pinch of salt over my shoulder.*

WH SMITH: Today, I saw not only a lemon-sucker but a mint-cruncher. Maybe it is in the staff handbook. Maybe it is compulsory.

I am too polite for my own good. There are so many things I want to say to these cretins (who, by the way, give the good customer service people an unfair bad name) such as: you have no idea how manically depressing it is that we have evolved from the same species; if idiots could fly, this place would be an airport; a mind is a terrible thing to waste and I'm glad they didn't waste one on you; I don't know what your problem is but I'll bet it's hard to pronounce. Of course, I keep these razor-sharp retorts to myself. But one day, maybe one day........!

MARKS & SPENCER: M & S is in the press for sparkling Christmas results. Congratulations to Stuart Rose and his team. I like the feel of Marks and Spencer but even it has more than its fair share of surly lemon-suckers. Maybe another big push on service will feature in the next phase of progress. Come to think of it, M&S hired a very expensive American guru to gee things up not so long ago, but in the several stores in my locality, service is still as mixed a bag as ever. It takes more than several suitcases full of dollars to change human attitudes.

OCEAN PEARL: We visited this local Chinese restaurant for a birthday meal. Everything was good from the warm welcome, the service, the food, the customer care, the free birthday round of drinks to the parting comments. It was a pleasure and a fine example of customer service as it should be with the customer, as the full focus of attention, being looked after by attentive staff. It was our first time at this restaurant and, you've guessed it, we will return. I remember a Chinese saying from a training course I attended years ago: "A smile will gain you ten more years of life."

DAY 11

WAITROSE: This is easily the best customer service I have ever had at supermarket checkouts. The operator was delightful. He hit all the right notes with body language, facial expressions, verbal interaction, help to pack and so on. As I left, I thought that if scientists could clone Dolly the sheep, then they must be able to clone naturally gifted customer servants like that. Silly idea, I know, but supermarket trainers and follow-up management must be able to get things right more often than not. So, why is service such a lottery? Anyway, the Waitrose guy is my new hero.

DAY 12

I wrote a blues song today about customer service and I even found myself banging it out on the guitar, when everyone else was out, of course.

LEMON SUCKIN' BLUES

"Woke up this morning, went to the store,
Wondering if I'd get a smile or frown at the door
I got the blues,
I've got them lemon suckin' blues
Will I win or lose
With those lemon suckin' blues

Shop girl smiles on the left,
Lemon sucker frowns on the right
I know where I'm heading 'coz I don't want a fright
With the blues
With them lemon suckin' blues
I want to win and not lose
With those lemon suckin' blues
I'll vote with my shoes
To sidestep those lemon suckin' blues"

The lyrics will not trouble the spirit of Muddy Waters but I got a few things out of my system.

DAY 13

SAINSBURY'S: Today at Sainsbury's, the checkout assistant was a mint-cruncher with lemon-sucking tendencies. Just before serving me, he popped an extra strong mint into his surly mouth. His manners were impeccable but his mush was a misery. There is an old one-liner: he was so stone-faced, a careers adviser encouraged him to apply for a vacancy on Mount Rushmore. Before I got to the checkouts, I do what I always do when shopping in food stores. I spend a few minutes watching staff handling fresh food – meat, fish, delicatessen, etc. – to monitor hygiene. I become like the obsessive-compulsive TV detective Monk when I witness the nose-wipers, hair-flickers, finger-lickers and face-scratchers continually failing to wash their hands. It is *the* food-buying turn-off and my horror applied not only to supermarkets and small specialist shops but also to catering establishments. My ultimate nightmare is the exposed salad bar, having observed several times in supermarkets, people sticking their fingers into the cous-cous mixture or, in one spectacularly vomit-inducing incident, an old drunk man scooping up potato salad with his bare hands and stuffing it into his messy mouth. Yuk. Today, bad hygiene was on display. So I bought pre-packed food that is probably just as prone to packers with bad habits handling it but there is some small comfort in the fact that I don't see the process.

Coincidentally, in today's newspaper there was a feature on hand washing. Apparently, the Scottish Executive has decided to spend £2.5 million on telling people how to wash their hands properly. At a conference some time ago, I was told that we spend too little time giving our hands a cursory wash and that we should use the time it takes to sing the Happy Birthday song to ensure we do a thorough job. It may result in you getting odd looks in the toilets, though. I award full marks to the Scottish Executive and more power to them as they take unnecessary flak for supposedly wasting money. The newspaper featured drawings of hands in various poses with excellent instructions: wet hands with water; apply enough soap to cover all hand surfaces; rub hands palm to palm; right palm over back of other hand with interlaced fingers and vice versa; palm to palm with fingers interlaced; backs of fingers to opposing palms with fingers interlaced; rotational rubbing of left thumb clasped in right palm and vice versa; rotational rubbing, backwards and forwards with clasped fingers of right hand in left palm and vice versa; rinse hands with water; dry thoroughly with towel; duration of procedure at least 15 seconds. That's not a lot of time but no-one can fault the need for more thoroughness. The next time I observe people in a fresh food environment washing their hands so methodically will be the first time. Hygiene in food businesses is just as much of a factor in customer service experiences as anything else. But, like the broad picture, inconsistencies dominate practices. Again, let the customer beware.

DAY 15

MORRISON'S: In Morrison's supermarket, the checkout assistant is deep in conversation with one of her colleagues on an adjacent till. I get no acknowledgement whatsoever. I might be invisible to her. Perhaps she has a rare eye disease and I am being unfairly impatient. Maybe I am a figment of her imagination or perhaps she is a figment of mine. Anyway, with her head cocked away from me and her hands sliding my few purchases down the conveyor belt, I notice a wasp landing on the back of her head. "Kill, kill," I ponder but the wasp flies away, probably hacked off that he too has been ignored. Finally, the assistant turns to me and says: "11.50." I look at her, waiting for some human kindness and basic etiquette but all I get is a brief blank look before she turns her head again in the direction of her colleague. Assuming that 11.50 is the amount of money I owe her rather than the time of the next train to La-la-land, I pay her. I leave without having heard a hello, thank you, goodbye, a wink of an eye or please call again. On my way out, I looked back and the assistant was still in conversation with her friend. I hoped that the wasp had gone to fetch a few mates before launching an assault.

NETTO: The back to basics, keep it simple, no frills approach of this store is commendable in many ways but there is no excuse for cutting back on personable, polite staff at the tills. How hard is it? They say any fool can be a critic. I know I can be accused of being both, but I am only critical about things that need criticising and lousy service is an easy target because there is so much of it around. Discounting prices does not automatically suggest discounted manners.

DAY 16

WICKES: I am not a big fan of DIY or DIY stores but such is life that every now and again I need to paint or fix or build or replace something. Today, I was looking for a new screwdriver. Once chosen, I took it to the checkout and witnessed the unacceptable face of customer service. There was no greeting, no eye contact, no interaction, nothing. I felt as if I was being processed like those people in 1960s Cold War movies when they arrive at foreign airports. It was a lifeless performance from the operator, uncomfortable for me and very, very rude. The only positive aspect of the whole experience was a reinforcement of my loathing of DIY and, especially, DIY stores.

DAY 17

ICELAND: Today I received just okay service in an okay shop from okay staff. Okay, but not nearly good enough. It's the kind of shop where you go in feeling good because the red colour scheme is bright and cheery but, a few steps in, one very quickly gets over it. There may be a massive suction extractor at the staff entrance draining employees of their natural personality and humour. Who knows? I might be right. The blast of hot or cold air at shop entrances depending on the season might just be some chemical to change personalities. I told a friend about this and he said: "But they have great prices and offers." Is that enough? Am I being unfair? Is service not as important as I think it is.

DAY 18

BBC RADIO SHEFFIELD: Buffeted by strong winds, soaked by cheeky rain taking advantage of my exposed head as I wrestled with my umbrella, drenched from the knees down by puddle water sent cascading by passing traffic on severely flooded roads, I arrived at Radio Sheffield feeling weather-beaten and a little apprehensive about a short recording on customer service I was doing for BBC Radio 4's "You and Yours" daily consumer show. But in contrast to the elements, the welcome from the receptionist was warm and helpful. I was shown upstairs to a waiting area and within minutes a studio assistant came out to greet me, provided hot coffee and eased my nerves with calming words. Handing in my visitor's badge on the way out, the receptionist, now joined by an equally friendly colleague, was still warm and pleasant, and bade me a fond farewell as I headed outside to the nasty weather again.

MORRISONS: A bacon sandwich came to mind, so I went to Morrison's restaurant. The girl on the till was a trainee but she did everything right – hello, eye contact, attentiveness, good parting comments. I have been to this restaurant before when the service was as chilly as an igloo's hallway, but today, on top of the BBC experience, was a great day for customer service, so far.

MARKS & SPENCER: What a day for superb service! It just gets better and better. In addition to the BBC and Morrison's, I can testify that the checkout operator gave the best service I have ever had in M&S. The customer service assistant was friendly, helpful, interested, with great eye contact, a pleasant manner and she helped with the packing without any prompting – excellent in every possible way. Note to M&S – more please. And, get this, her name was Verity, which means truth and if ever there was a truer example of excellent customer service personified, this was it! Pity the misery on the adjacent checkout didn't follow the example of his neighbour. I have made the point before – same company, same recruitment process, same training but different outcomes. How come?

DAY 19

SAINSBURY'S: This morning, as I waited at the checkouts, I began to think about a conundrum. What would you get if you merged the Keystone Cops with headless chickens? Answer – the supervisors in Sainsbury's today. Some days, the checkout queues flow reasonably well but days like today are just too frequent. 75% of the checkouts were closed. 75%!! Slowly, extra help was drafted in via manic tannoy calls but a sophisticated business like Sainsbury's should be better prepared and react faster to their customers' needs. I wasn't the only one tutting. Sometimes, it's good to tut.

DAY 20

THORNTON'S: Into this chocolate world for a coffee, but unlike the confections on offer, the sweetness had not penetrated the steely features of the service staff. I know that making coffee in these places is a big task – it takes ages – in a steamy atmosphere, but service should not be this half-hearted. It was a nice Americano with chocolate chip, though, despite the assistants with the shoulder chips.

DAY 21

MATALAN: Here is a store with one of the longest runs of tills I have seen in a clothing emporium but why oh why oh why am I forced to stand in a queue of seven people with only one till open? It beggars belief, but it happens almost every time I go into a Matalan shop anywhere. The service itself is pleasant enough, but by the time it gets to your turn, you are wound up and don't really appreciate the efforts of the person behind the counter.

DAY 22

UPPER CRUST: It was a bitterly cold Monday morning and, according to the papers, the most miserable day of the year – Blue Monday – as people are faced with awful weather, Christmas bills and broken New Year resolutions. All of that might explain the Upper Crust railway station snack bar assistant's frozen face when I asked for a coffee. There was zero warmth, no eye contact and as much personality as the cold sausage sandwich on display. She looked as if her hobby might be stepping on garden rakes. As I studied the menu to decide which size of cup and blend of coffee I wanted, she rolled her eyes in her solid face and, one step away from spitting venom, was silently urging me to hurry up. I watched her from my table as she served other customers and wondered why she was hired in the first place – one for the lemon-sucker's hall of fame.

VIRGIN TRAIN: The train manager/ticket collector was excellent in every way. He was an informative, calming, professional voice on the tannoy as he gave us general information. In person as he clipped the tickets, his manners were impeccable, as was his eye contact. Now it is obvious why he was hired – because he's a natural for customer service.

BIRMINGHAM STATION: The ticket checker on the gate must be related to the Upper Crust assistant – glum and no interaction whatsoever. He had that kind of Eeyore look. The man on the information desk, however, was great – friendly and helpful. I suppose you've either got it or you haven't.

HUDSON RECRUITMENT: In the outer reception, the man on the desk was first class – nice welcome, nice manner. The Hudson receptionist was equally warm and hospitable. On the increasingly rare occasions I come across exemplary service I am reminded that it can be done. There are just not enough customer servants willing to devote – yes, devote – themselves to the whole service vocation.

EAT: In for a coffee to ease the chill – a polite but soulless coffee shop with not a trace of a smile from the service assistants. I am convinced that a lot of employees just as they are about to go through the workplace entrance, park their personalities, sense of humour and manners outside and then perform a Jekyll and Hyde swap before they start work. So far today I have experienced the very best and the very worst kinds of customer service – inconsistency rules, it seems!

I listened to BBC Radio 4's "You and Yours" in a Birmingham side street and was very impressed at how well they polished out the ums and aahs from my piece. I think the point of the broadcast came across ok but my little jab at Post Office service struck a raw nerve with listeners. A few e-mailers wrote in to support their local Post Offices but my stance is not to have a go at all Post Offices, merely to reflect my personal experiences of the ones I use regularly. I might concede that small village or rural Post Offices with a regular clientele might give a warmer, chummier service than a big city unit, but as far as I am concerned, the jury's out. It is great to get a reaction from listeners but, grateful as I am, I would prefer reaction and, indeed, action from Post Office managers to sort out their service.

The Daily Express listed 10 steps to happiness, not unlike the other formula earlier this month – try something new; get physical; contact a friend of relative you may have lost touch with; take a break; be nice to a stranger; help the planet; pamper yourself; plan something new; go to the beach (ha, ha – on this day of all days when shipwrecked containers have been spewing salvageable goods onto a beach in Devon); share your thoughts. An alternative strategy would be to look in the mirror and simply say: "Smile, damn you, smile!" I am reminded of the old joke advising that if you want to wake up with a smile in the morning, go to sleep with a coat hanger in your mouth.

DAY 23

MARKS AND SPENCER: My local Marks and Spencer is a nightmare for checkout service. There are never enough tills opened up and the manager always seems oblivious to customers waiting. But today, the checkout operator seemed to be in the witness protection programme because she was wearing a baseball cap with the peak pulled down hiding her eyes. Now, as a retail veteran, I know that one of the most important things in customer service delivery is eye contact, except I suppose if one is on the run from the Mob. Maybe this assistant had one yellow eye and one purple one, perhaps she had embarrassing wild bushy eyebrows or maybe she had fallen for the old workmates trick of putting superglue around the rim of her hat. Whatever reason she had, this customer was not impressed, and the manager was standing just three feet away. To be fair, it might be a new initiative from M&S on their environmental crusade. Maybe too much eye contact is bad for the ozone layer and I am just being a sad, impatient, miserable example of a customer for not realising and misunderstanding.

DAY 24

HMV: Some record shops and most sports stores have the selling space versus customer browsing space ratio all wrong. HMV today is a case in point. I am sure if I had not been jostled and interrupted as

I browsed that I would have bought several items. But, after about ten minutes, I left the shop in frustration. Shops selling books, CDs, DVDs, computer games, etc., surely must realise that people like to take their time to look around the merchandise, but sometimes it is impossible. I wonder how many sales are lost because of basic space management indiscipline.

DAY 25

TESCO: Today seemed to be rugby training day in Tesco. As I walked along the aisle, I could see a Tesco assistant aiming herself in my direction but with her eyes fixed on something or someone behind me. She seemed unstoppable and intent on getting through a space, no bigger than a gnat's windpipe, between a fixture and me. She slammed into me, stopped, looked up at my aghast expression and muttered sorry before proceeding on her mission to kill. The customer is always.....a punchbag?

DAY 26

WATERSTONE'S: Like libraries, quite a few bookshops are breeding grounds for lemon-suckers and today I could not have been served by a more miserable human specimen. She said all the right things but it was obviously a burden to her. I was tempted to drag her to the self-help section but I decided that a miracle was needed to inject some sparkle into this deadbeat.

DAY 27

SUPERDRUG: Here is the usual nonsense – four tills available, one open and a queue of seven people. The assistant was both efficient and sullen. I sang silently to myself: "I'm not a lemon-sucker, I'm a lemon-sucker's son and I'll keep on sucking lemons 'til the sucking season's done."

CONNAUGHT HOUSE: We waited at the till point for about four minutes without any sign of staff anywhere in this kitchen shop, and then left without buying anything. Perhaps it was one of those new shops where, instead of everything being priced at £1 or some other dirt-cheap price, everything was free. Who could tell? Who cares?

BOOTS: I picked up a couple of tins of shaving foam and walked to the tills only to see a massive queue and, surprise, surprise in the High Street, some tills closed. I put the tins back on the shelf and on the way out I noticed signs saying "Change One Thing". I thought about screaming: "Yeah Boots, change one thing, open more tills."

WAITROSE: Here was a refreshing example of plain, old-fashioned courteous, friendly service from a young man on the baskets-only checkout. He shone through on a not untypical day of inconsistent service. You see, people, it can be done. It really can.

DAY 28

WH SMITH: It must be a company policy but instead of saying "hello" or "good morning" or even "wotcha, man", WH Smith's staff wherever I go always mutter the same opening gambit "Do you want a bag?" Now I know the environmental spin and the cost-cutting reasons behind this tactic but does it have to be the first and in a lot of cases the only words spoken by WH Smith's employees? "Would you like a bag, sir?" might be more polite. "Hello" would be even better. Pigs might fly.

DAY 29

TISCALI: I telephoned the customer service number to query a problem with my telephone bill. Over nine months ago, I changed my telephone provider from Tiscali to the Post Office, on the understanding that the Post Office would communicate with Tiscali to arrange the transfer. Since April 2006, I have been getting line charge bills from Tiscali and on checking my annual accounts, I realised that direct debits had been paid unnecessarily to them, amounting to nearly £100. After a few minutes, I spoke to a customer service assistant who was calm and collected as he listened to my woes. My suggestion was that if Tiscali checked back, it would be as plain as the nose on an anteater's face that I had no call charges on my bills for almost a year and that they should refund me the money I paid them. The assistant sounded unsure of his ground and put the onus back on me to get proof of the transfer from the Post Office, which I should then send to the customer services team at Tiscali's head office. I asked for the name of someone to whom I should send the proof but he told me just to address it to the customer service team. He was polite but not terribly helpful on what was a fairly straightforward problem in my opinion.

POST OFFICE: Re the Tiscali business, I telephoned the Post Office number and was knocked out by the warm, friendly, helpful voice of the girl at the other end. She listened, was empathetic, helpful and just about everything you want a call centre operative to be. She said she would do her best to resolve my problem, assured me that she had sent an email to the appropriate person whilst I was on the phone and gave me the impression that here was efficiency and care personified, if not facially, at least vocally. It remains to be seen if the problem will be resolved quickly and satisfactorily. When I put down the telephone, I thought for a second: why can't post office counter staff be like the person I had just spoken to? If you can smile with your voice, you can smile with your face – obvious, but not always done.

DAY 30

HOTPOINT: I telephoned the spares centre to enquire about high temperature glue for an oven door and the customer service assistant could not have been more professional, friendly and helpful. The order was placed, now let's see how long it takes to arrive.

WAITROSE: The customer service centre called back to thank me for my complimentary feedback which I had sent to them following a recent visit. It made me think about customer complaints and from my experience as a customer servant, it is a general rule of thumb that complainants are more likely to be offered gift vouchers or other goodwill gestures because they are unhappy and need to be pampered, but satisfied customers expressing delight are thanked and that's about it. There is something screwball about that but he/she who shouts loudest in life invariably gets some pacification reward. It is no wonder some people in this irritable society can see gold in grumpiness and in the gullibility and weaknesses of companies. But that aside, well done Waitrose.

DAY 31

HOTPOINT: Ta-daa! The glue arrived – excellent and efficient service. Mind you, £12.99 for a tube of glue when I only needed a couple of squirts is not economical. The chances of ever using the rest of the glue are pretty slim. But a little devil on my shoulder has some ideas the next time a checkout operator forgets or is determined not to smile!

DAY 32

Ah ha! It is reported that *Which? Magazine* surveyed customers regarding their opinions on shops and shopping, with John Lewis as favourite and Aldi and Lidl beating the big supermarkets. The survey covered product, convenience, service, pricing, shopping experience and the resultant overall satisfaction percentage. But in the context of this diary, I was interested in the customer service numbers. John Lewis, the winning company, scored 67% for customer service (i.e. 33% dissatisfaction), Waitrose scored 71% (i.e. 29% dissatisfaction), M & S scored 49% (i.e. 51% dissatisfaction) and Waterstone's scored 53% (i.e. 47% dissatisfaction). It's all proof that inconsistency is the reality of customer service. As customers, should we just accept it in our weariness or is the fight worth continuing?

DAY 33

A by-product of my observations on customer service is people-watching generally and whilst I maintain that it is right to criticise poor service, it is also right to be appalled by the behaviour of some customers. We live in an era of selfishness, bad manners, grumpiness and bullying. To service employees, a queue is a lottery – never knowing the mood and personality of the next customer.

That is why it takes a certain type of person to be a great customer servant. Some of the customer antics in various shops in town today were appalling. I keep being reminded as a retailer and as a customer that the customer is not always right.

DAY 34

CURRY'S: We went to Curry's in search of a new vacuum cleaner. I must admit that electrical shops frighten me a little because they are tangible exhibitions of the sprinting pace of technological progress. We wanted a Dyson vacuum cleaner but isn't it a testament to brand brainwashing that we still refer to these machines as Hoovers? We looked around and were approached by an assistant. My wife asked to see a plugged-in demonstration and as the assistant lifted down the display model, she muttered to herself that there seemed to be bits missing. She plugged in the machine and struggled to find the switch to power it on. Another assistant, possibly the manager, swept past and hit a button, without stopping and without acknowledging us. My wife "Dysoned" a bit of the carpet and then asked to see another model in action. There was something incomplete about that one as well. The assistant was helpful enough, but lacked product knowledge and warmth. As my wife enjoyed the demonstrations, I had a chance to observe the other staff. A young blond service assistant was draped over the back of a male assistant who was tapping something into a computer. Later, as we waited at the cash desk to buy the Dyson, I noticed the same girl behind the counter asking if anybody had any headache tablets. She was leaning against the desk and seemed to be flicking something from her hand in the direction of yet another assistant. Even though she was not serving a customer directly, she was presenting a bad image of Curry's — lazy and careless. Who hired her? Who is managing her? Who is training her? Who has the guts to tell her she is not suitable? All in all, we got what we wanted but customer service delivered in a professional manner, with personality, was sadly lacking and it was no wonder that Curry's only scored a low percentage for customer service in the recent *Which?* satisfaction survey.

DAY 35

Today, wandering around a market, I looked at some of the miserable stallholders and thought of that great Klinger line from MASH: "If my dog had a face like yours, I'd shave its butt and train it to walk backwards." There is a kind of romanticism about market traders but some of them forget the basic ingredients of great service.

DAY 36

STARBUCK'S: Another coffee shop, another long queue, another long wait for a fairly simple cup of coffee, a limp hello, no thank you and a pretty dismal level of efficiency and service overall.

DAY 37

I am reading Jeremy Clarkson's book, "And Another Thing", a collection of his columns and was struck by his line that "shopping can never be a pleasant or worthwhile activity." Obviously, he is in his provocative, grumpy guise here, but he is both right and wrong. Of course shopping can be both pleasant and worthwhile, but the phrase just exposes the inconsistencies in shopping and service generally. In the same way that companies kid themselves that they can deliver on the premise that the customer is always right, customers have come to expect, wrongly, that their shopping experience will be guaranteed as pleasant and worthwhile or else somebody's ear is going to get chewed off at the customer services desk. In the same way that I believe customer servants should be hired more scrupulously and paid much higher wages, I contest that customer expectations should be lowered – under-promise and then attempt to over-deliver, not the other way round.

DAY 38

TESCO: When you have two checkout operators working on adjacent tills and they insist on chatting to each other throughout your transaction, ignoring your very existence, you wonder why Tesco is as successful as it is. Today, this very thing happened and these two operators must have come from the same mould because they were gum-chewers as well. I must have given the operator serving me a scowl of a look because she gave me one back. I thought about saying something to her but I reckoned that I might end up as the villain of the piece if I really spoke my mind. Here was a classic case of me, the customer, doing a bit of calm shopping only to be frustrated and wound up at the tills. Someone once said that to shoppers the first impression of a retail store is important and so is the last. In most cases, car parking issues aside, the last point of contact is at the checkouts, so why are badly trained or badly managed or badly recruited people put into these important ambassadorial positions? The answer my friend is blowing in the wind because it keeps happening, and not just at Tesco.

DAY 39

RENAISSANCE HOTEL: I arrived for an appointment and enquired at the reception desk about the person I was meeting. From that moment, I was extremely impressed with the wonderful service and helpfulness demonstrated, not just by the desk assistant, but also whilst I was waiting in the lounge area, by the restaurant manager, the coffee bar waitress and various others who glided through the lounge/reception area. I noticed particularly that as soon as a hotel employee had dealt professionally with a customer, they continued to look relaxed and genuine after the customer had left. In so many places, the smiles when they are on display are welcome enough, but the instant face-change as soon as customers turn their backs smacks of a less genuine approach to service. But this hotel was demonstrating something very special indeed in its approach. I sent an email via the Renaissance/Marriott website to the customer care link. From bitter experience, as I mentioned earlier, I know that complaints far outweigh compliments.

DAY 40

I nipped into a little newsagent – I forgot to look at the name on the fascia – and the lady behind the counter was delightful. That's it.

DAY 41

SAINSBURY'S: On a busy Saturday morning, as ever, not all checkouts are open. But, as I have a basket, I head for the "baskets only" till to find it closed. Next to it is the "10 items or less" till. I have 11 items, but I join the queue. The lady in front of me seems a little anxious as she counts the items in her own basket. She too has 11 and looks round. She says: "Oh, I'm sorry, I seemed to have more than 10." I replied: "Don't worry, I have more than 10 as well, but what's the worst that can happen?" She looks around again and says: "They might tell us off." I smile and tell her not to worry. We both get through without a telling-off. But I decided to drop a line to Sainsbury's to gain an understanding of why all the checkouts aren't opened on busy Saturday mornings, especially both the "baskets" and "10 items" tills to rattle through the customers with only a few items. And why do they cause anxiety to some customers by hanging up unnecessary signage?

RENAISSANCE/MARRIOTT: This is the reply to yesterday's email compliment: "Thank you for contacting Marriott. We appreciate your kind message regarding the exemplary service you received while staying at the Renaissance Hotel. We appreciate the time you set aside to share your experience. Exceptional associates who exceed guest expectations are a source of pride at Marriott. Individuals such as the staff at this hotel truly define the tradition of exceptional service Marriott strives to maintain. We are forwarding your comments to associates in the Executive Office at the property to ensure that your positive feedback is shared with these associates. We appreciate your continued patronage and value your opinion." It is a nice, prompt reply, but a little too verbose and fancy, perhaps. I think this was sent from a US location and that might explain the flowery language. And I am not entirely comfortable with this trendy challenge for businesses to come up with alternative words for employees and staff. Some use "associates", others use "colleagues" and I seem to recall Disney refers to "cast members". They are all hired hands however they're described. It is all in the service not the fancy names. But, well done to the Renaissance Hotel.

DAY 42

NATIONAL TRUST CAFÉ/RESTAURANT: A long queue, eventual cheery service from the girl taking my order and surliness from the coffee-maker. Here were two employees about three feet apart, different as chalk and cheese. Fancy that.

DAY 43

POST OFFICE: The same old story as twelve people queue for four open service-points in a seven windows operation. Again, there was plenty of time for observations and, unsurprisingly, everyone supposedly serving looked bored, unhappy and loyal to the lemon-sucking standards of misery. There was even a gum-chewer behind one of the windows. As customers approached the windows, I could see that normal procedure was for the service assistants to look up, not say a word of welcome and just wait for customers to speak first. It was as wrong as bad service can be. Ironically, I noticed one of the Post Office's current promotions to do with personalised stamps. It is called "Smilers".

SAINSBURY'S: I received this email response to my recent complaint about checkouts: "Thank you for contacting us. I am sorry to hear that your recent visit to our store was not enjoyable. I note from your email that not all of our checkouts were open on the Saturday. I can understand how frustrating this must have been, especially as the store was particularly busy that day. I have spoken with the store manager, who has asked me to pass on his apologies to you. He has advised me that there has been an increase in staff illness. This combined with Saturday being the busiest day since Christmas and other issues, resulted in the long queues and lack of checkouts open. He has also advised me that the '10 items' checkout is available for customers who have few items who wish to get through the till quickly. However, on a busy day, cashiers would not count the items being put through and would not differentiate between 10 or 11 items. Our aim is to try our best to help our customers as much as we possibly can. If you have any further concerns about this or any other matter, please feel free to ask for the store manager the next time you are in store. I know he will be more than happy to discuss them with you to ensure your future shopping experiences at Sainsbury's are much more enjoyable. I have arranged for 1,000 points to be added to your Nectar card as a gesture of goodwill along with my apologies. This equates to £5.00 and will be available within the next 72 hours. I hope you will be able to use them to purchase something you particularly enjoy next time you are in store. Thank you once again for taking the time to contact us. Your feedback is much appreciated." This is a nice and prompt enough response but as a customer it might be interesting to know about a shop's absenteeism problems, but when I am queuing I simply don't care about that. There are enough people in supermarkets working behind the scenes to come and give support to checkouts at busy times. The "10 items" checkout business is exacerbated by the hanging sign above the conveyor belt and the assurance from the store manager that the checkout assistant will not differentiate between 10 and 11 items is a bit of a gamble for customers wary of breaking the rules. The solution, to avoid customer versus customer potential conflict, is either to remove the sign completely or to put up another sign saying "basket only" or "approximately 10 items". In short, the onus for customer service decisions should not be dumped onto the customer.

DAY 44

LIDL: I read today that triskaidekaphobia is the name given to the fear of the number 13. As I stand in a queue, I ponder if there is a word for the fear of long and hard-to-pronounce words and a fear of being blown away by unexpected perfect service. I think I am going mad.

DAY 45

TESCO: The assistant on the kiosk was glum, the server at the fish counter was lovely, the shelf-filler who escorted me to the light bulbs was perky and the checkout assistant could not care less – is it me?

DAY 46

BANNATYNE'S HEALTH CLUB: I nipped in to ask for membership information to be greeted warmly by the smiling receptionist who could not have been more welcoming. Another assistant came out of an office to speak to me and, again, the personality and professionalism was exemplary. The information was clearly explained and the complimentary cup of coffee went down a treat – excellent.

ASDA: This is one of the smaller Asda stores and, as such, some of the aisle widths are a bit narrow for passing trolleys and static browsers – a not uncommon problem in High Street shops, especially sports shops, where the idea to is squeeze in another fixture or display a feature in an already cluttered area. It makes for a frustrating shopping experience and denies customers their "proper" share of space. However, my main beef with this trip was the checkouts and the checkout assistant. In this supermarket, there were thirteen checkouts, seven were open, and therefore six were closed. I heard a tannoy message calling for assistance, as the area was getting quite busy. No-one seemed to turn up to help in my time there. Eventually it was my turn to be served. The checkout operator did not look at me nor say hello. I think I was awarded a brief eye-blinking glance as I was asked for payment. At the end of the transaction, the operator failed to look at me again and did not muster any effort to make a parting comment – no thank you, nothing at all. I thought Charlie Chaplin would have made more noise at the height of his silent movie career. What struck me about this, apart from the obvious lack of customer care and downright rudeness was that its US owners now heavily influence Asda. Wal-Mart prides itself on its customer service standards. This example today showed that there is still work to do – and anyway, in my couple of trips to America, there is just as much inconsistent US customer service delivery as there is in the UK.

DAY 47

ASDA: In contrast to the smaller Asda, this is a hypermarket and to counter the poor service in the smaller store, the two employees who helped me whilst shopping were superb. The checkout operator was great too from the welcome to the parting comments. It may be ageist and politically incorrect to even think it in these litigious days but all three of the Asda staff were mature ladies. Does that make a difference? It shouldn't but it might. It did today, anyway.

DAY 48

MORRISON'S: I enjoyed my shopping from start to finish. Everyone was helpful and polite. Easy, peasy, but very, very rare.

DAY 49

SAINSBURY'S: My earlier observations about the "basket only" and "10 item" checkouts, commented upon by Sainsbury's reply, took a little twist this morning. Neither checkout was open and when I asked a passing supervisor why, she said it was because she did not have the staff yet but they were due in soon. Before I had reached the checkouts, I had noticed several staff members who could have been "borrowed" for a quarter of an hour to open a basket checkout, but it seemed that it was okay for customers to wait for the next shift of staff to arrive for work. Is it me? Try something new? I might try a different shop.

DAY 50

On the basis that solitude is more enjoyable if you have someone to share it with, I start the day with the ambition that I will not encounter any queues today and I end it by lowering my expectations considerably. Perhaps we should just expect to wait and, therefore, by lowering our expectations, we will be a much less stressed, tolerant and happy society. I did avoid queues and stress because I did not do any shopping at all.

DAY 51

SERVICE STATION: I could have been the invisible man as I handed over my payment. The assistant looked through me and did not utter a sound.

DAY 52

THE THREE HORSESHOES: This pub in a thatched village looked inviting enough as we stopped off for a lunchtime snack. With that wonderful real-fire smokiness in the air, we stooped to enter the cosy lounge. The greeting from the landlady was a little lacklustre, but not offensive. The waitress was dispassionate, mechanical and routine but the speed of service and food quality was excellent. If only the "olde worlde" charm we felt on entering the village and the warmth of the beamed lounge had been matched with a much more relaxed and inviting human response. Perhaps, working in a pub day in and day out takes its toll on the human spirit, and eventually on the quality and genuineness of customer service.

HEVER HOTEL: This was to be our base for a few days. The receptionist was cool in the temperature sense but efficient. What you want after a long journey is your host's wide smile and jolly demeanour to give you a hug of a welcome. As this is partly a timeshare location, within minutes of arriving in our room there was a sales representative at the door insisting that we must attend a breakfast meeting with him to discuss options. We declined, but he insisted. We declined, but he insisted again. We declined and, flustered, he said that he might have to come back to get us to sign a form confirming his breakfast invitation and our decline. We said OK and off he toddled.

Sunday night in the small towns of Kent trying to find a pub serving food was like searching for the Holy Grail blindfolded. I remembered another expression when trying to locate something – it is like a blind man in a dark room looking for a black cat that isn't there. We tried three pubs and each time the landlady looked in disbelief, as if I had just trod on their cats, and almost enjoyed telling us that, fool, the kitchens are closed on Sunday evenings. Instead, we were forced to settle for a menu of deep-fried anything we wanted at a greasy takeaway. We opted for two pieces of fried chicken, we think, for the species was unidentifiable, and fries, along with a bottle of wine from the off-licence across the road. That night we feasted in our room watching Top Gear. Bliss.

DAY 53

STABLES RESTAURANT: Our first breakfast here and we experienced very cheery but exceedingly slow waiting staff. There was no orange juice at the buffet table and a refill of the jug took ages to arrive, slightly longer than it took to replenish the empty coffee urn, but slightly less time than it took to bring some cups to the table but a tad longer than it took to get clean knives and forks. The cooked breakfast was excellent.

DAY 54

STABLES RESTAURANT: This morning's breakfast experience was a "groundhog day" repeat of yesterday, unbelievable but true. Customers' huffs and puffs added an interesting soundtrack to the two waiting staff running around.

DAY 55

STABLES RESTAURANT: Breakfast is such an important meal, or so we are told. It is also one of the simplest meals and therefore difficult to mess up. Breakfast here is a buffet table of cereals, fruit, urns of hot drinks and baskets of butter and preserves. Today the service was tortoise-slow and our table was not set with any cutlery. The waiter forgot to bring salt and pepper when the table was set eventually, butter was missing from the buffet table and the orange juice jug was down to its last dregs. In other words, it was a case of poor preparation, lethargy plus little attention to detail resulting in bad service. When service is this pedestrian, customers tend to restrict what they order off the menu, tending to opt for relatively easy choices. This morning, there were plenty of waiting staff causing draughts as they raced about doing things not directly related to specific customer service needs. Some Americans on an adjacent table had fixed bemused smiles throughout the time we were there.

DAY 56

POUNDLAND: Brilliant service!

DAY 58

SAINSBURY'S: A rather large poster in Sainsbury's says that every time we re-use a carrier bag the planet says "thank you." I make a note to contact Sainsbury's for a tape-recording of the planet speaking.

DAY 59

Keeping a diary of customer service allows an opportunity not only to study customer servants but to observe customers too. There is plenty of mileage in the exposure of surly and grim shop assistants et al, but some customers display such appalling behaviour that sometimes it's no wonder that customer service assistants react in kind. Today I heard a customer, as he walked out of a greetings card shop, call back to the assistant inside: "You should be a bit more bloody polite and respectful, you silly cow." I thought a) that sounded out of order no matter what happened and b) ironic, because surely respect works both ways. Anyway, a few steps further on the man tripped on a cracked paving stone, stumbled and wobbled a bit before he regained his composure. Chastened? Somehow, I doubt it.

DAY 60

NEXT: What a bland, unresponsive customer service assistant. I could not believe it.

DAY 61

The London Paper published my guest column on tipping:

"To tip or not to tip, that is the dilemma. A tip is always expected – ask any taxi driver – but not always deserved. Is tipping just a duplicitous way to supplement low wages? The customer seems to be expected to pay extra for this thing called service, regardless of standards,

especially in restaurants. Recently, a group of us went out to a pizza restaurant. The food was fabulous but the service was a little slow, a tad robotic and littered with several mistakes – forgotten starters, wrong wine, etc. As a group we put in our share of the bill and I took it to the cashier. We had decided to leave the change as a kindly tip. Standing next to the till was the restaurant manager who watched the money being handed over and, in a mechanical calculator kind of way, he quickly worked out the change amount as a percentage of the total bill. As soon as I had generously said "keep the change", he glared at me with a death mask stony face and said: "That's only 8%. Isn't that a little insulting to your waitress?" I stood with my friends in a collective dumbstruck rigidity before saying: "The food was great but the service was just okay. Our tip reflects the service." He continued to glare and complain about our stinginess citing at least 15% as a starting or indeed tipping point. We stood firm and left the restaurant wondering why we felt like naughty schoolchildren. This kind of pressure happens all too often either from the management or from the hangdog waiting staff who are only interested in supplementing their meagre wages. Here's a warning notice I would like to see outside restaurants: "THIS RESTAURANT DEMANDS THAT YOU AGREE TO PAY ANY SERVICE CHARGE WE DECIDE TO PRINT ON YOUR BILL AND IT WANTS YOUR GUARANTEE THAT YOU WILL TIP WAITING STAFF WITH AN AMOUNT NOT LESS THAN 12.5% REGARDLESS OF THE STANDARD OF SERVICE." This is not about meanness nor is it meant to sound grudging or tight. If I want to leave a tip, I will leave a tip of my calculation and choosing. If I feel that it is not deserved, then it is my right not to leave it. Come on restaurateurs, pay a decent wage rate to your staff and encourage genuine tipping as a pure bonus to the people who really deserve it."

So there! My wife thinks I'm just being mean and miserly in my attitude to tipping but, like unnecessary queuing, it winds me up.

DAY 62

The London Paper's readers' reaction poll to my column on tipping – 91% said "more" and 9% said "bore". My son remarked that it was a landslide, which, of course, it was. One correspondent wrote that if service is rubbish, no-one would go back, so there is no need to tip. If it's good food and service, tip a little and return to give the place the benefit of any doubt. If the service is exceptional, tip appropriately and become a regular customer. I agree up to a point. But I still maintain my stance – why tip anyway?

DAY 63

MARKS & SPENCER: We queued at the express checkouts (irony!) and felt a bit herded as we trundled through. This is the same branch where I experienced the best M&S service I have ever had. Today was average, not insulting in anyway, but delivered in a blasé way by an assistant who seemed keen to get her next tea-break.

DAY 64

MARTIN'S: I was buying a magazine and somehow felt throughout the transaction that I was interrupting the conversation between the two assistants. How rude of me.

DAY 65

STATIONERY BOX: There were two people behind the service counter. One guy looked as if a fox had just eaten his lifelong pet rabbit whilst the other was brighter (maybe she owned the fox) and did all the right things except smile convincingly. I know I bang on about it but here we go again, same company, same recruitment process, same training, different outcomes. Bizarre.

DAY 66

HILTON HOTEL: I paid £3.75 for a large Americano coffee that took ages to arrive, served by a young lady economic with her facial and verbal expressions. I wondered if she was renting the space in her personality vacuum as it could be quite profitable. Am I being too hard on people?

DAY 67

WH SMITH: It is the same old apathy. I keep giving them chances but they keep failing. I used to buy most of my newspapers, magazines, books and stationery from WH Smith but I am getting very close to abandoning them altogether. How can a chain of shops get service so wrong most of the time?

DAY 68

SAINSBURY'S: Gadzooks! It was a case of well-organised checkouts, a happy operator and efficiency all the way. Is this the beginning of a new era or a fluke? Watch this space.

DAY 69

POST OFFICE: Horrible, horrible, horrible! As usual.

DAY 70

PUBLISHERS BOOK CLEARANCE: "Hello. It's me, your customer. Excuse me, would you mind paying me a tiny wee bit of attention while you serve (ha, ha) me? I'm not really interested in the minutiae of your lives. There are two of you. Could one of you at least acknowledge my presence?" Two wastes of good retail oxygen employed to tolerate the paying public stood side by side, engrossed in their own solar system, talking about some party the night before. I felt like saying: "It's been lovely but I have to go outside and scream now."

DAY 71

One of the newspapers recently ran an article on a submission to the Competition Commission's enquiry into the grocery sector by, well, God, or more precisely from the Diocese of Exeter on His behalf. The submission accuses supermarkets of embracing environmental causes to persuade their customers that they are the best things since sliced bread rather than destroyers of rural and urban communities. The reference to God reminded me of a piece I wrote recently about religion and supermarkets. I was researching some material for an article on the power and influence of supermarkets when, in the background, I heard an old favourite record on the radio. It was "Deck of Cards" by Wink Martindale, which was a top ten hit in 1959. (Picture the scene in his agent's office at the beginning of his career: "We gotta get you a humdinger of a name, kid – Colin just ain't showbiz enough – now, how about Blink, Glance, Squint, Bat, Flicker, Twinkle? No, no, wait, I've got it – Wink!") It is a wonderful tale of a soldier's use of his deck of cards to remind him about God, the Bible and prayer.

The story involves a group of soldiers who go to church and, on the instructions of the chaplain, they refer to their prayer books, except one soldier who produces a deck of playing cards. The platoon sergeant spots the soldier and arrests him for playing cards in church. Hauled up before the troop commander, the soldier is given an opportunity to explain himself and launches into a spirited defence by saying that each card reminds him of a religious message. He says that the ace indicates only one true God. The two illustrates the old and new testaments of the Bible, the three suggests the holy trinity, the four recalls Matthew, Mark, Luke and John, and so on. He finishes his explanation to the commander by noting that not only is the deck of cards a substitute religious aide-memoire, it is also an almanac of sorts – there are 365 spots in a deck of cards, the number of days in a year, 52 cards, the number of weeks in a year, 4 suits, the number of weeks in a months and 12 picture cards, the number of months in a year. Anyway, the commander swallows it, the soldier gets away with it and it all ends happily. If you have not listened to it recently or, worse, if you have never heard it at all, do yourself a massive favour and seek out a copy. It is as corny as the Jolly Green Giant's larder but if it doesn't change your life, it will certainly make you a far nicer card player, bringing out a much less aggressive approach to Snap and Old Maid.

I thought about the "Deck of Cards" when writing the supermarket article and began to think about these great commercial cathedrals and the millions of discerning customers who trudge up and down the aisles in search of cabbage and custard, healthy option yoghurt, kipper and puy lentil preserve and baked beans with octopus – you know, the kind of people who like to spice up their mundane shopping trip for carrots and milk with that little something different in a defiant shopping strategy that screams out "I am not like the rest of you in the sauces and pickles aisle. I have my own identity." The deck of cards idea struck a nerve when associated with a shopping list. Instead of church and supermarket in conflict over who gets the most people through the doors on a Sunday, it seems to be a distinct possibility that both camps can work hand in hand to maintain our moral fruit and fibre while we are searching the breakfast cereal shelves. Supermarkets spend a lot of time and resource researching the customer experience and they frequently refer to "the customer path", a route around the store for a typical shopping trip. It starts with the parking space and finishes on the other side of the checkouts at the end of the visit. In other words, like life itself, supermarket shopping has a beginning, middle and end. If we substitute the deck of cards for a shopping list, we can all learn lessons and be reminded of our reason for existing every time we go shopping.

When I look at the trolleys, I know that there will be some with wonky wheels, a reflection that in life not everything is or can be perfect. I gaze in wonder at the array of fruit and vegetables and marvel at the iconic images present in potato skins, faint outlines of faces staring back at me with eyes drilling into the core of my humanity. My compassion as a human being is drawn out when I spy an ugli fruit and I pray that one night the greengrocery angel will transform its rough and unattractive exterior into the smooth and unique persona of a butternut squash. I look at pizzas and I see various ingredients co-habiting their round world together in complete harmony, with the possible exception of anchovies, but as with the wonky trolley wheels, even pizza world has its downside. It is easy to get cheesed off when things get a little crusty. The butchery department displays steaks to remind us of our stake in the well-being of society, chickens to encourage us to break free from our cooped-up existence and run out there in the free-range of life, egging each other on to better things and offal to help us to remember that no matter how awful life can be at times, no matter how much of a stew we get ourselves into, from all those entrails and tripe, something wholesome can emerge. On and on we go into more obvious territory with the freshly baked bread of life, the milk of human kindness and no peas for the wicked.

It is all there for us to study as we shop. No longer do we have to adopt our robotic approach to supermarkets. It can be the new university of life, full of joy, full of learning, full of inspiration and full of positive messages. See your shopping list in a whole new radiance. Take heart from the "Deck of Cards" message, from the blessed Wink Martindale, from the powerful supermarket machine which up to now has sapped your resolve. Take the family with you to the supermarket, take your neighbours, take the whole street. Together, in the cosy world of luncheon meat, cheesy puffs, cream crackers and Marmite, there is hope for mankind in the very place where we thought it could never happen. You see what a long career in retailing can do to a person!

DAY 72

I came across this quotation from "Wealth of Nations" by the great philosopher and economist Adam Smith: *"To found a great empire for the sole purpose of raising up a people of customers may at first sight appear a project fit only for a nation of shopkeepers. It is, however, a project altogether unfit for a nation of shopkeepers, but extremely fit for a nation whose government is influenced by shopkeepers."* Such is the strength of retailing and, inherent in that notion, the power of customers.

DAY 73

LOCAL COUNCIL: These days, there are a lot of stories about over-officious local authorities. One area of authority stamping is where people should position their wheelie bins before the refuse collection operatives (I am playing safe here and not calling them bin-men – oops!) arrive. Now, call me old-fashioned but rate-payers are customers of local authority services and as such require some level of customer service. So, when the council expectation is for a bin to be parked within an inch or two of a driveway, for example, why do the jolly (I am being sarcastic) operatives leave the emptied bind yards away from the original position, sometimes blocking the pavements. Some service, eh?

DAY 74

THE LOW WOOD HOTEL: What a great welcome from the receptionist – warm, polite and helpful. The room was full of charming little touches including a jar of sweets, bottled mineral water, a range of hot drink sachets and just a feeling of professional housekeeping standards and attention to detail. Later, I discovered that my mattress was a water-bed, a mild shock at first when I climbed into it and the whole thing wobbled. It was actually quite comfortable as I drifted off my moorings and sailed into the deep slumber of dream world. Great service, and a little mattress motion, if you know what I mean, calms a person.

DAY 75

THE LOW WOOD HOTEL: In contrast to yesterday's receptionist, this morning's automaton was as devoid of human interaction as a tin of soup. Smiling was obviously off his agenda, but maybe he had a headache or had financial problems or was worried about the melting icecaps or was just a grumpy so-and-so – who knows?

BURGER KING: I stopped at one of those appalling service stations where the car park is not maintained, potholes seem to be an accepted part of the landscape, and weeds and litter appear to be planned decorations along the footpaths and steps. The maintenance of places like this is just as important a part of customer service as the transaction process, but a lot of managers fail to make the connection. There are some service areas that I refuse to frequent for this very reason. Am I in the minority? The Burger King was the main part of a sad-looking room and the grunting approach to customer service from a "hello mate" kind of guy seemed to fit into the miserable surroundings. Another lad was exactly the opposite of a well-groomed, efficient-looking individual – you know, the kind of person that should be fronting a catering service. His long, untidy, greasy hair had escaped from his filthy baseball cap and his lolloping manner suggested that he had been employed to fill a vacancy quickly and trained for about ten seconds on how to fry the chips. A couple of times whilst waiting for the food to cook, he took off his disgusting cap and ran his hands through his horrible hair. He and his colleagues were the unacceptable face of food service and hygiene and a) had I not been very hungry and b) because any germs on my food would have been deep fried and massacred, I persevered, ate quickly and, like Butch and Sundance after a bank robbery, I got the hell out of there. Ugh!

BP FILLING STATION: It was just like the moon – no atmosphere. No small step towards any attempt at customer consideration, one giant leap into the gaping abyss of inconsistent service. It was a pleasure to drive away, watching the BP sign decrease in size in my rear-view mirror.

DAY 76

ICELAND: The manager's name, apparently, is Sharp. I ponder: sharp, as in on-the-ball efficiency sharp or lemon-sucking sharp. The latter seems to reflect his face and the general mood of the store today.

DAY 77

The Chief Executive of Debenhams is quoted as saying: "We continue to expect the retail environment to remain challenging." Phew! It's tough being a CEO having to come up with deep, inspirational statements like that. I think I'll file it with all the other statements of the bleeding obvious. The government has decided to increase the minimum wage to £5.80, slightly better than before but still laughable as many hourly-paid service staff will still be paid a pittance for the huge responsibility of delivering customer service. I remember years ago debating this point with a company director during a conference coffee break. Well, he almost choked on his custard cream and said the idea was ludicrous and would never happen. I fear he might be right. Customer service employees deserve much more and customers certainly warrant higher investment but, sadly, there goes another flying pig.

DAY 78

RYMAN'S: What a pleasure! The service was polite and helpful. Why can't other companies push the envelope (ho, ho) on service like this?

DAY 79

OLIVER'S: There is still something romantic about the notion of a small town tea shop full of homely people waiting to welcome weary travellers, and nutritious local menus to sustain them for the next leg of the journey. But this place on this day was staffed by a model lemon-sucker clearly made to look even droopier, I imagined, by the thought of carrying that face with her for the remaining days of her wretched life. Her companion in this unwelcoming, unwholesome enterprise was conversing with a couple of American visitors and seemed to be trying extremely hard to show how wonderful we all are in this green and pleasant land because her forced laugh at every comment sounded like a cross between the worst shrill you can imagine and a Gatling gun in full throttle. The food was good but it was refreshing to hear the door shut behind me on the way out. And no, I didn't leave a tip.

DAY 80

MORRISONS: What a chaotic shambles of a checkout operation! A clump –or whatever the collective term is for a group of checkout supervisors – stood still for what seemed like a long time as queues increased. Occasionally, one of the clump would crane his neck or point at something in a bid, perhaps, to give waiting customers the impression that things were about to improve. I estimated that a full 50% of the checkouts were closed and, my favourite hobbyhorse, the "baskets only" till was allowing trolleys through. Aaaaaarrrrggghhh!

DAY 81

PAPERCHASE: It is quite funny, when you are not in any kind of a hurry, to observe sales assistants lost in a daydreaming trance, completely oblivious to the real world around them, in a kind of peaceful place where the general public are banned from entering. I watched one such person today for a few minutes before leaving the shop, unacknowledged and untroubled for a possible sale.

DAY 82

POST OFFICE: Although, on the outside, I remain quiet, I hear my inner voice screaming: "HEY, I AM NUMBER THIRTEEN IN THIS QUEUE AND YOU HAVE ONLY TWO WINDOWS OPEN. ARE YOU HAVING A LAUGH BECAUSE WE'RE NOT?" Good grief.

DAY 83

BOOTS: I was on very good form today, upbeat and happy. Sadly, the checkout assistant in Boots was just the opposite. Think of the merry banter we could have had with our electrifying chemistry. We will never know. I reckon there must have been some potion or other on the Boots shelves to perk people up a bit.

DAY 84

MARKS & SPENCER: On a recent trip to a M&S store, I pointed out to a member of staff that the fresh food chiller tops were filthy with dust and other debris. I followed up my comments with an email to the M&S website. The manager responded thus: "Firstly, thank you for your email. I can fully understand your concerns regarding dust and debris on the tops of our chilled cabinets and I fully agree that this is not acceptable. We do have a detailed cleaning programme that has obviously failed to reach the correct standard. I have spoken to both my store team and our contract cleaning company and we have agreed that this situation must not be allowed to happen again. We are starting to clean these fixtures from today and all tops will be cleaned to the correct standards on a cyclical basis. Thank you for raising this issue and I hope you will continue to enjoy shopping in Marks and Spencer." This is exactly the response I would have expected – reassuring, humble – but without a hint or word of apology. It is one thing to have a detailed cleaning programme but if this same store manager is not using his eyes on several daily walks around the shop, then he needs some managing himself. Fresh food stores in particular need impeccable standards, otherwise customers will lose trust and then it is the slippery slope.

DAY 85

TULIP INN: What is this? It is a hotel with a very welcoming receptionist, a great room, efficient (perhaps a little overly so at times) restaurant and bar team, not bad food and slick and efficient checking out procedures. Blimey, it might catch on all over the country. But I am still hearing oink noises in the distant sky.

DAY 86

McDONALD'S: I am not a fan of fast food but it has its place, I suppose. The restaurant was busy and the team behind the counter was running around in a strange blend of efficiency and mania. The pace was blistering and a manager, I assumed, was orchestrating things very well. I noticed how all the assistants, one-on-one with customers, presented themselves calmly and politely with all the heat and frenzy around them. They were doing a great job.

DAY 87

COMET: I was told once that it is important for a shopkeeper to make the most of every customer that walks in. No-one told the staff in this Comet store. There was a bunch of staff behind a counter, a lot of loud talk and laughing but not a scintilla of effort to mix with customers. I was in the mood to buy a new laptop but I walked out, as I was not going to part with my money if they did not seem to be interested in my presence.

DAY 88

SAINSBURY'S: This is one of the smaller, local shops and the customer service assistant informed me that they had run out of plastic carrier bags but I could buy a bag for life. I said I did not want to buy a bag and how was I expected to carry seven or eight items without a carrier of some sort. She stood firm. I told her, as calmly as I could, that I would leave my shopping and go elsewhere. For the want of a few pence, Sainsbury's lost a sale. I know that some people will see my action as petty, but I get irritated by little annoying things like this.

DAY 89

GATEWAY HOTEL: The first thing that hit me when I was entering this hotel was the cigarette fug lingering in the area just outside the door, and the first thing that hits a smoker is, I suppose, a sense of gagging relief that they can puff here until their hearts and lungs give out. As one of the non-smokers, I detest smoking (thank goodness for the law) and it would be a good enough reason for me never to return to this hotel, had I not been on a two-day training course. I realise there is a big debate between puffers and non-puffers, but that's another diary, perhaps. Another thing that was quite off-putting in a service sense, apart from the staff who failed to acknowledge or engage with passing customers, was the lunch buffet at nearly £8 per person. It consisted of a round of sandwiches each, a bowl of coleslaw, a plate of nacho chips, fruit, chocolate dessert and hot drinks. I thought it was in the Dick Turpin league of great highway robberies of our time. Hotels are part of the hospitality industry, but this one seemed to have opted out today.

DAY 90

GATEWAY HOTEL: Ditto.

DAY 91

WH SMITH: A gum-chewing girl is talking to her mate about shoes as I am being (pardon me for using the "s" word) served. I look at one of them and then the other but I felt as if I was interfering in their conversation. I hoped they would buy the highest heeled shoes possible and then fall off them into oncoming traffic. I am joking. I meant to say a herd of marauding elephants.

DAY 92

SAINSBURY'S: Blimey! Heavens above! Fireworks, please! No checkout problems today. Hooray!

DAY 93

SAINSBURY'S: The checkout assistant would have been perfect if cast in a remake of "Bad Day At Black Rock", all stern and serious, a face frozen in contempt. Yesterday was great. Today just grated.

DAY 94

BP FILLING STATION: A robot served me today – at least I think it was a robot because no flesh, blood and personality entity would have been so clunkily mechanical in a service (yes, service) station.

DAY 95

STARBUCK'S: The young lad who took my order for a croque monsieur panini was great but the young lady who eventually served it was guilty of wasting her make-up on that day because, clearly, she did not want to be working here. No amount of cosmetics could have hidden her true feelings. The quick mouth-twitch smile from glum to smirk to glum spoke volumes.

DAY 96

One of the papers lists ridiculous job titles, an indication of the tendency of employers to use more and more complicated words to describe simple jobs: Domestic Engineer (housewife); Knowledge Navigator (teacher); Flueologist (chimney sweep); Stock Replenishment Adviser (shelf stacker); Head of Verbal Communications (secretary); Petroleum Transfer Engineer (petrol pump attendant); Cash Relations Officer (banker); Crockery Cleansing Operative (washer-up); Space Consultant (estate agent);

Media Distribution Officer (paper boy); Foot Health Facilitator (chiropodist). God help us all. I think the time inventing new names could be better spent making Customer Service Assistant work in practice, consistently.

DAY 97

INSTORE: I bought a 99p watering can, was served with courtesy and a smile and called "sir" as I was thanked for shopping at Instore. Well done! I have lost count of the times I have spent hundreds of pounds, and on a few occasions thousands of pounds, without a sniff of a sincere thank you.

ICELAND: I read yesterday that Malcolm Walker, the CEO of Iceland has led quite a recovery and, along with other senior executives, will share £60 million in incentive payments. It's a pity that almost every time I shop in an Iceland store, the checkout service is sluggish and half-hearted. Whatever financial success Malcolm Walker is enjoying should be compensated with a truly monumental push on customer service standards and checkout management. Mr Walker was one of a number of CEOs who, last year, failed to respond to a letter of mine. But am I bitter?

DAY 98

BIRD'S: This is one of the busiest butcher's shops I have been in with plenty of staff bustling about behind the counter and butchers cutting and chopping away. The service is more efficient and businesslike than warm and welcoming. But it seems to work.

DAY 99

HMV: There is a tendency for record shop employees to be a bit too cool in their dealings with the public. The urge to look casual and hip, not to smile unnecessarily and to mumble rather than speak clearly was borne out today as I purchased a Haydn CD for my wife – classical music but not classic service.

DAY 100

HEALTH CENTRE: I telephoned for a repeat prescription and the Dalek on the other end took my details and hung up. They must be sick of sick people.

DAY 101

HEALTH CENTRE: I arrived to collect my prescription and, without looking up, the assistant asked me my name and if I had a reference number. I gave my name (for I am not a number, I am a free man). She thumbed through the pile of prescriptions, asked me to confirm my address and then thrust the piece of paper in my direction. I took it, readied myself for a steely glare back at her, but her head stayed bowed. Customer service counts, even, perhaps especially, in health centres. This was just plain rude.

DAY 102

One of the papers listed the ten most intelligent non-human primates – orang-utan, chimpanzee, spider monkey, langur, macaque, mandrill, guenon, mangabey, capuchin, gibbon, woolly monkey and baboon. I think this intelligence is going to waste and that these primates should be hired by some customer service businesses to improve interaction. I know I am being a cheeky monkey.

DAY 103

ICELAND: In the middle of the afternoon, I queue up as usual to pay for a few things and judder in shock at the sight of two young guys sitting on the window ledge inside the store drinking from cans of lager. Several times the checkout assistant looked over at them but there was no hint of calling for security or the manager to eject them. It cannot be a new customer service policy surely. As I left the shop, I noticed a group of four security guards from this and other stores having a smoke and a chat in a doorway. Customers should all feel safe.

DAY 104

WH SMITH: I asked for sixty first-class and sixty second-class stamps. Panic at the tills! They hadn't enough stamps at this paypoint. The assistant bellowed to her colleague to get more stamps. The minutes ticked by, I eventually got my stamps but not one word of apology for the delay. This seems to be standard service for WH Smith – the customer always seems to be a bit of a nuisance.

MOLONEY'S: Here is a good-looking butcher's shop with a great display of meat. The service is warm and helpful. That is it, plain and simple service with a smile. No lemons being sucked here. They could teach WH Smith staff a thing or two.

DAY 105

GREENWOOD'S: This men's clothing shop – mainly for the older gentleman based on the merchandise – is old-fashioned service personified. The female staff member is warm and friendly and the male assistant is energetic and fussy, matching ties to shirts and jackets to trousers in the true spirit of salesmanship. It's a throwback to another era but, based on most service standards in the same street, it is a wonderfully refreshing experience.

DAY 106

SAINSBURY'S: It is announced that Sainsbury's will have a "no carrier bag" day next week in a new twist on environmental policy. The puff is that Sainsbury's issue and we use far too many plastic carrier bags that are not biodegradable. Fair enough, up to a point, but the real reason is surely their selfish intentions to cut carrier bag costs and increase profits. The green spin is just the gloss of pompous self-satisfaction. Supermarkets thrive on reading the moods of the nation and jumping onto bandwagons to suit their own needs. There is nothing wrong with that but why do they have to be so pious about it? Watch out for the next big thing and observe supermarkets jump ship onto to another passing fad. Oooooh missus, how dare I question environmental policy!

DAY 107

MARKS & SPENCER: I paid a visit to the M&S Shop where I witnessed the filthy chilled cabinets and discovered that despite the assurances by head office and the store manager, not much had changed. So I emailed this letter: "A few weeks ago I wrote to bring your attention to dirty chiller cabinets at your store. Today, my first opportunity to revisit, I was appalled at how little cleaning had taken place despite your assurances and those of the store manager that a cleaning programme was in progress. The management of the store must be walking round with their eyes closed. Look at the tops of the cabinets and the more visible rims above the top shelves! It's so obvious it's embarrassing. I would have expected an "all hands on deck" approach to hygiene and an urgency to clean the cabinets thoroughly over a weekend. But, hey, I'm only a customer! You'll tell me I'm important, but I'd rather you proved it. As a customer, I object to being fobbed off and duped and I would rather see actions than read ineffective words in a standard letter. I'm sorry M&S, the old arrogance regarding customer feedback appears to be seeping back in to your operation and I feel my trust in your company dwindling, after more than 30 years as an advocate and as a loyal customer. I like your products but I don't like this attitude. If I'm lucky, I might get another letter of false promises and platitudes, but I'd rather see immaculate chiller cabinets – that's, of course, if I ever bother to visit this store again." This is the head office response: "I'm sorry to hear that you have not seen an improvement on your most recent visit to one of our stores. I can assure you that such matters are of the highest priority to Marks and Spencer and we do not like to hear that we have fallen below the high standards we set. I can only apologise if you feel fobbed off or duped by the initial response you received. However, it is extremely useful for me to have received your email and I will ensure your comments will be shared with the manager at the store. I know they will share our concern to hear your comments and address the matter." Here's my point – if these matters are of the "highest priority", then why was nothing, or not much, done to clean the place up? Blah, blah, blah!

I could go on but one hundred and seven days should be enough to make a point or two.

Someone else's one hundred and seven diary days would be different, but I am reasonably confident that whilst experiences may not be the same, inconsistency in customer service delivery would be a common agreement. The point about a diary like this is to record and then reflect on the many examples of customer service and customer treatment, and my conclusion is that, generally, service delivery ranges from average to dire. There are a few wonderful examples of exemplary customer servants but, sadly, there are not enough of them doing this important work. Business managers can spend hours preaching and discussing the theory of customer importance but in practice there is still much to be done to improve customer service at the point of delivery. Retailers are amongst the most influential people in society because they have vast experience and expertise in gathering information on trends but their failure to find solutions to inconsistent service standards and flawed staff selection should astound all of us. It should also spur companies into action to have another go at solving this most basic of business requirements.

Ssssssssssh! "Retail Confidential" home truth alert:

There are too many uninterested, lazy, bad-mannered, unsuitable people in customer service positions. Is it their fault? Maybe, to some degree, but the bulk of the responsibility for wrongly selected employees in these crucial jobs lies with managers who, by their weaknesses in judgement, are showing major deficiencies in themselves. Companies are weaker as a result and, as a consequence, customers are being denied consistently high standards of service, despite marketing hype, costs of recruitment and, sometimes, condescending lip service.

6

HOW CUSTOMERS FANCY THEMSELVES AS COMEDIANS IN HOW THEY ACT, WHAT THEY SAY AND WHAT THEY EXPECT

As promised, here is a selection of other true tales from my retailing past. For sheer amusement, I have exaggerated some of the stories, but I guarantee that in essence they happened and I apologise in advance for some of the puns. Remember from the previous chapter that it is my contention that the customer is not always right. I offer the following exhibits, M'lord.

THE ATTACK OF THE BLEACH BOTTLE

In a large hypermarket, no two days are the same, and that can be both a good thing and a bad thing. Sometimes a manager just wants a quiet life but as soon as the doors open and customers arrive to shop, all bets are off. Thankfully, most customers are legal, decent, honest and truthful and just get on with their shopping, but every now and again, something happens and a customer tries it on, thinking that he or she can make a bit of money on the sly.

One day I was called to the customer service desk to speak to a young man. As I approached, I could see that he was not happy about something or other. He told me – and I have not changed his words – that as he was walking down one of the aisles in the shop, a bottle of bleach just jumped off the shelf and splashed all over his leather jacket. He actually said the bottle of bleach had *jumped off the shelf*. I mustered all of my professionalism and good manners and apologised, but on inspection of his jacket, I explained that most of the wear and tear could not have been caused by the alleged incident. He left unhappy, but without a penny, a chancer who took a chance and failed.

As incidents like this are always worth following up, like a good battle-worn manager who has gone a little stir-crazy, I went to the aisle and gave all of the bleach bottles a good talking to, but rather like the man with the leather jacket, some of the bleach was too thick to take it in.

HOW CURRY CAN BE A WORRY

It is easy for customers to get hold of the wrong end of the stick, (or the twig, or the branch – all will become clear as this story unfolds). I was having a coffee break one morning in my office, away from the shenanigans on the shop floor, when a young mother phoned to tell me that, in her words, there was *a tree* in her curry ready meal. I sat in my office, phone to ear, quite shocked at this strange complaint but, like the TV cops of the 1950s, we managers are always trained to get the facts, Ma'am, just the facts. But I couldn't help but imagine a giant oak firmly embedded in amongst the chicken, peppers and curry sauce.

As I was concerned, I asked her to bring the offending meal back to the shop and she agreed to come in that very afternoon. But as soon as I had put the phone down, I realised that I had not offered the services of a lumberjack and a large truck. But, as it happened, none of that was necessary. When she brought the curry meal in, I unwrapped it and found *two bay leaves* in the exotic mess. I explained that bay leaves were there to help flavour the food and she reddened up and laughed. "But it's still part of a tree," she said. "Yes, it is," I agreed, "but, thankfully, not the whole tree." She ignored me, accepted a refund and left the shop. I thought about this complaint for a while and concluded that in this game, sometimes life is not fir, but we can all pine for a better fuchsia, and no matter what, it is important to curry favour with all customers when they korma round to my shop.

HOW THE JOHN WEST WAS WON

Health and safety concerns have seeped into our heads, sometimes for good reason and other times causing overreaction. One day, I was getting ready to go home after a long day, when I received a call from a man, clearly distraught. His voice was a mixture of panic and anger. He said that his family had eaten salmon sandwiches for their tea and his wife and son had found pieces of glass in amongst the fish. I was taken aback. This was a new one on me. After he assured me that his family did not seem to be suffering from any ill affects at this stage, I offered to send someone round to his house to investigate. But he declined, saying that he would bring the remainder of the sandwiches and a newly opened tin of salmon to the shop straight away. I agreed to meet him.

At his request, we met in a private office and he produced the sandwiches and opened salmon tin. "There," he pointed, "glass." I studied the fragments carefully, touching one or two with my finger before using my thumbnail to crush a piece of the glass. I then proceeded to taste the white powder and I could hear the man gasping in disbelief. "What are you doing?" he spluttered. "Oh, just tasting some rock salt," I said, trying not to sound too smug. "It's natural in some tins of salmon." I could see the man's dreams of compensation drain away with the colour from his face. He coughed a bit and then rushed off to explain things to his anxious family. Later, I reflected that it's important to stay in tuna with your customers even if some of them act like pilchards.

THE PRINCESS AND THE MILK-SHAKE CARTON

It is not often I can remember the exact dates of customer complaints but 6 September 1997 stands out because it was the day of Princess Diana's funeral and a quite bizarre incident happened. In order to give everybody a chance to watch the funeral on TV, all shops closed on that morning. Later, at two o'clock, we reopened and within ten minutes, I was called to see a customer. As I got closer, I noticed red mist around her head, cheeks a-flush, hands on hips and a trace of steam coming out of her ears. I detected she was annoyed about something. (Now bear in mind the sadness of the day.)

"I am furious," she began. "I have just driven my new car into your car park and I drove over a McDonald's milkshake carton, causing the contents to splash out all over my new tyres. What are you going to do about it?" I stood staring at her like a rabbit locking onto the full beams of a juggernaut, my face frozen, and wondering if I had just heard what I thought I heard. She looked at me and said, with menace, "Well?" My head was searching for the number of a psychiatrist or a hit man. Eventually my mouth uttered an apology and an offer of a free car wash. She demanded the full wax and polish and I thought but didn't say, "Yeah, first the car and then you, baby." I agreed to her demands and she stomped out of the shop. As it was raining, I was doubly cheesed off but I went out in my big mac to retrieve the milkshake carton that had caused the McFlurry. The woman who had made an unhappy meal of it had gone. It had been a burger of a day.

THE HIGH SCALLION JOB

(Note: Some readers might not know that a scallion is Irish terminology for a spring onion and that champ is an Irish recipe of mashed potatoes, scallions/spring onions and butter – for this story took place in Belfast.)

Customers come in all shapes and sizes, from all backgrounds, as do shoplifters. A shop is a thieves' paradise and professional bandits know all the tricks of the trade to confuse and distract, as they attempt to steal anything that is not nailed down. They are a menace but, the more inept thieves, the ones that have more than enough empty space between their ears, the ones that aimed low in life and missed, provide some light relief. One day, we followed a man who was wearing a long overcoat. It was one of the hottest days of the year and he looked as out of place as a kipper in a tap-dancing class. By the fixed smile on his face and his glazed eyes, it was obvious that he had lunched recently with Jim Beam or Johnnie Walker. He was high as a kite. Slowly but surely, he walked around the shop putting various things into the pockets of his coat. After about half an hour, as he was about to leave, we apprehended him and took him to the security office.

"Please empty your pockets," I said.

"What pockets?" he slurred.

"The ones in your coat."

"Oh, those pockets," he chuckled.

In a few minutes, the following items were displayed on the desk: a bottle of brandy, a packet of custard powder, two small tins of cat food, a bar of chocolate, a bag of sugar, a bottle of ketchup and a bunch of scallions. The man was arrested and whiskeyed off to the police station, leaving us wondering if all the food and drink he had tried to nick had been intended for a romantic meal for two – or just a quiet night in with the cat. Even with the scallions, he was more chump than champ.

THE LAG WITH THE BAGS WAS A DRAG

Nowadays, people who use plastic carriers bags are marked out as environmental terrorists, threats to the Solar System and swans, horrible human specimens who should be taken to a dark room and flailed every hour on the hour with whips crafted from bags for life. But, about ten years ago, we got used to the fact that five minutes before we closed our shop, the same customer, a middle-aged, scruffy man, engulfed in his own stale body odour, would come in every evening without fail to pick up last minute food bargains. At the checkouts, he insisted that each item was to be wrapped in a separate carrier bag and then all the individual bags were then to be gathered into one outer bag. At the end of a long day, this routine was as welcome as breaking wind in a spacesuit. But, with the highly dubious mantra "the customer is always right" rattling around our addled brains, outwardly we remained calm and professional but internally we were hiring imaginary assassins to take him out as soon as he stepped into the car park. We were convinced that he was not a sufferer from obsessive compulsive disorder because of his grubby appearance and his horrible, nostril-recoiling, unwashed stench that was the exact opposite of Chanel No. 5. We were convinced that he was a nuisance. One evening, I decided to ask him about his carrier bag quota. Holding my breath for as long as I possibly could between questions, I eventually found out that he was using the plastic bags to repair several leaks in his roof. He said he was damned if he was going to pay to have it fixed and that our bags were the best solution he could find. We never did discover a way of reducing his carrier bag quota and we had to console ourselves with the fact that we were caring for a member of our community. In fact you could say that he was enthusiastic and bombastic in his use of plastic to take the fantastic but drastic roof repair action and that it was easy for us to be sarcastic and inelastic in our judgements.

CSI: CUSTOMER SCENE INVESTIGATION – RETAIL'S MOST WANTED

As I have illustrated, customers come with different personalities and motives. It is useful to expect the unexpected, especially the different types of customer likely to walk through the door and in my experience, here is how I would classify them:

- **The Sprinter** – the one that comes in, chooses, buys and leaves without catching a breath
- **The Browser** – the one that seems to be killing time but just might part with their money
- **The Decisive Buyer** – the one that knows exactly what they want, mind already made up
- **The Ditherer** – the one that needs equal measures of attention and product knowledge
- **The Silent Type** – the one that chooses to be uncommunicative
- **The Talker** – the one that loves to chat and chat and, er, chat
- **The Distrusting Customer** – the one that reckons retailers are disreputable
- **The Know-all** – the one that cannot be told anything new
- **The Obnoxious Kind** – the one that is always out for confrontation
- **The Sweetheart** – the one that is an absolute joy to serve because they are no trouble

Ssssssssssh! "Retail Confidential" home truth alert:

It is okay to laugh but many retailers, managers and employees forget to do it and forget how to do it. It feels good and in appropriate circumstances, it is a great release. It is a serious business but it does not have to be morbid. Next time you are in a shop, ask to see the manager. When he or she appears and says: "How can I help you?" you respond by saying that you would like a darn good laugh, please. The look on his or her face should do it.

7

HOW RETAILERS HIRE THE WRONG RECRUITS AND RISK DAMAGING THEIR BUSINESS

I have worked in retailing when staff turnover – people leaving the business – has been as high as 30% in some parts of the country and although those employees resigning give various reasons for leaving – bad management, low wages, boredom, opportunities for new beginnings, marriage, moving house location, etc. – a huge problem originates, in my view, back at the recruitment and selection stages. Some people leave businesses for good, sensible, positive reasons but many leave because they have not been recruited, trained, managed or cared for properly. There are too many of the wrong types of personalities drifting into retailing having been allowed to slip through the net by amateur or lazy assessors.

In modern human resources, there are so many sophisticated methods of assessment and selection that, in theory, it should be impossible for anyone unsuitable to be offered a job. But I have witnessed many times the scrambling around of HR managers trying to get a team of assessors together and, sometimes desperately, grabbing the first person to pass their desks, regardless of experience or ability in this very specialised and critical area. Sometimes, assessment centres are run brilliantly, but far too often they are a hot-potch of dangerous amateurism. The candidates looking for a job are unaware of these deficiencies, of course, because they assume that everyone running the day is a first-rate, bona fide professional. The reality is that quite a lot of recruitment decisions either way, job offer or rejection, are made by the wrong people for the wrong reasons. So therefore it is no wonder that staff turnover is so high.

In my experience sometimes the human resources function tends to attract the wrong kind of person to its ranks. I am not talking here about the eventual shop-floor recruits but about the recruiters themselves. As I indicated, I have been on dozens and dozens of assessment and selection days and conducted or assisted in hundreds if not thousands of job interviews, witnessing first-hand the good, bad and ugly sides of hiring.

Human resources management concerns itself with finding, developing, motivating and retaining human resources to keep businesses running. It also has responsibility for nurturing company cultures, evolving working atmospheres to allow commerce to function and people to perform well and to flourish. There is clearly an onus to train and to provide fairness, legal protection and a degree of welfare. It is a formidable list of tasks and despite the occasional emergence of a true "people person", sometimes these tasks are managed by unqualified managers who happen to have "drifted into" personnel as transients on their career paths. The effectiveness of this type of manager who is just passing through rather like a cowboy drifter in a western town can be tantamount to a lottery draw when it comes to influence. But, I will come back to the management floaters later when I describe some assessment centre recruitment days. For the moment, I would like to concentrate on career "people managers" and look at a couple of examples of style.

I will talk about a human resources manager called Cruella – obviously not her real name, but a moniker that suits her harsh manner and approach to managing people. By contrast, I will also discuss another HR professional, Teresa, mother figure to her team, a person who empathised with and took a personal interest in her employees.

Cruella was a career personnel manager. She had been doing the job in various locations for more than twenty years and she was often described by her peers and subordinates as "old-school", some would say a dragon, but by George I am too much of a gentleman to endorse that view. She developed a management style throughout her career where she made no bones about who was boss – she was. It seemed that she had forgotten how to smile and her body language made everyone in her presence feel uncomfortable. But she knew every detail and procedure in the world of human resources. She was sharp mentally as well as vociferously, and she was brilliant to have on your side in a crisis, e.g. a disciplinary or dismissal situation. Her record-keeping and general administration were immaculate. The staff in her own immediate team and those in the wider shop environment were wary of her and could not find one iota of warmth towards her. Work was certainly more efficient but morale was very erratic, leaning on the unacceptable side. So in this example, is it right to have a people manager razor-sharp on policies, procedures and legalities or a person as cold as a Polar bear's bottom?

Now Teresa was loved by just about everyone in the entire store team. She came across as a sincere, empathetic, approachable, friendly and helpful people manager. Like Cruella, she was adept and more than competent with policies and procedures, displaying efficiency and effectiveness in her job. The morale measurement of the business showed very good results, an indication of a happy team, by and large. The big difference between the two styles was time management. Cruella was as strict about her diary control as she was about human resources administration, and she had the added advantage, bizarrely, of a cold personality that dissuaded people from dropping in to her office for a cosy chat. Teresa, on the other hand, adopted an open door policy whereby anyone could come to see her without an appointment. She maintained that a people manager had to be available for the people whenever she was needed. Cruella, on the other hand, always made appointments in her diary. So which idea was best? I am tempted to mimic comedian Harry Hill and say "there's only one way to find out....fight!" But we are professionals here.

The truth is that both approaches work and a lot depends on the working environment and atmosphere. Sometimes slack businesses need someone tough to come in and crack the whip a bit until standards and processes are raised to an acceptable level. At other times, some businesses thrive on a softer more endearing approach. But the one certainty is, particularly in this litigious era, that whoever the people manager is and what his or her personality may be, they must be on top of their game when it comes to HR procedures, legal obligations and administration. The warmth of personality, it seems in business, can be seen as an optional extra.

I have taken three random examples of Human Resource Manager recruitment advertisements to illustrate a couple of points. These are actual examples with some slight editing to maintain anonymity.

Recruitment advertisement example 1

"The ideal candidate will have a focused commercial approach to HR to deliver tangible results that will shape and drive the business forward from a people management perspective. You will provide and deliver an effective employee relations service with a clear and extensive understanding of current employment legislation and possess a thorough understanding of performance management – linked to behaviours and how these affect objectives and outcomes. You will also oversee current recruitment programmes. "

Recruitment advertisement example 2

"HR generalist responsibility for a business employing 110 full and part-time staff; managing the compensation and benefits structure and the annual pay review process; managing the annual performance appraisal review process; developing the company's learning plan via personal development plans; working with partnerships to provide strategic HR input and leadership; monitoring and relaying information on key performance indicators (KPIs) such as employee satisfaction and retention; managing all personnel administration including contracts, holidays, sickness, etc; championing the Investor in People accreditation to add value to the organisation; ensuring talent management and succession planning policies are in place."

Recruitment advertisement example 3

"Act as a stand-alone HR Manager with complete autonomy to drive the HR function both in terms of operational and strategic HR; identify synergies within other divisions and perform responsibilities related to: the design and implementation locally of global HR strategies; the planning, organisation, direction, control and monitoring of employee relations; supporting and providing direction in compensation matters; the recruitment of personnel; the training and proactive development of employees and other activities as directed by the business unit and/or company. You will work closely with the senior management team to analyse and diagnose business issues and ensure visibility of related HR issues, risks and opportunities. We are looking for an experienced HR professional who has experience of operating in a multi-site environment. You will have previously participated in the development and negotiation of bargaining agreements and have worked with unions to facilitate change in attitudes."

It is easy to see that the technical skills required are paramount in each of the examples, and in my illustrations previously, Cruella and Teresa could both fit the bill. But it is interesting to me that the advertisements – again, I stress they were picked at random – seem to ignore the humanity inherent in the term people management. We read about the importance of driving business and achieving tangible commercial results. We see the litany of HR technicalities from a "people management perspective", (rather like a sniper on a watchtower, perhaps), including something called "HR input" in the "HR function". There is mention of investing in people, recruitment, performance appraisals, training, proactive and personal development, succession, employee relations, legislation, behaviours, objectives, outcomes, synergies, strategies, risks and opportunities, all important stuff when managing people in the modern business climate. But, for me, there are two things missing from these advertisements. Firstly, there is no warmth in them regarding empathy, welfare and compassion. Where is there any mention of the importance of people to an enterprise? Where is the element of flesh and blood to emphasise the critical presence of this key, living, breathing ingredient in business success? It all smacks of trying to sound hard and tough, focusing on ability rather than affinity, and all three advertisements just sound incomplete and unbalanced to me. All three miss the vital point of such a job role – the human element, the people part.

Secondly, having chosen not to include the human in human resources, the advertisement copywriters, or whoever devised the scripts, also failed to state any requirements whatsoever about the personality or characteristics of the type of person they were looking to recruit. Arguably, they could have – should have? – included a passage on relationship-building, ability to connect with others and, here's a clumsy phrase but I hope you get what I mean, commercial kinship, i.e. working together, with all the intrinsic emotional and practical connotations for a common cause. Cruella or Teresa? Who has the HR X factor? Press the red button or text your vote now. Here is my list of the important areas of talent a human resources manager must have:

- A sincere and genuine welfare interest in people as people rather than as statistics
- Organisational expertise to encourage a climate of integration and cooperation
- A believer in employee participation
- An evangelist for the clearest possible communications culture
- Design ability when it comes to creating job specifications
- People planning skill to maximise labour requirements for optimum business efficiency
- Recruitment and selection decisiveness to choose the right people
- Skills in performance appraisal and job evaluation to maintain quality
- Passion for training and development to secure the business's future
- A policing discipline for employment practices and industrial relations.

I am sure you can think of other aspects and definitions but the important thing to remember is the people part of people management and the human part of human resources.

I remember a colleague telling me this very funny story – remember humour is in the eye of the beer holder – related to HR, which I note here as a kind of natural break before we move on to some aspects of recruitment. The joke is in the form of an email from a boss to the HR department.

TO: Human Resources Department
FROM: Derek Hartley

Arthur Jones, my Administration Manager, can always be found hard at work at his desk. Arthur works as a driven self-starter, without wasting company time talking to colleagues. Arthur never thinks twice about helping his team mates and he always finishes projects and assignments on time. Often Arthur takes extended measures to complete his work, sometimes giving up coffee breaks. Arthur is an individual who has absolutely no vanity in spite of his high accomplishments and profound knowledge in his field of administration. I firmly believe that Arthur can be classed as an excellent, highly competent employee, the kind that cannot be dispensed with. Consequently, I hereby recommend that Arthur be promoted to executive management, and my proposal for this will be executed as soon as possible.

Thank you and best wishes,
Derek Hartley
Arthur Jones's Line Manager

This email was followed up within minutes by a second missive from Arthur's line manager:

TO: Human Resources Department
FROM: Derek Hartley

Arthur Jones was reading over my shoulder while I wrote the report sent to you earlier today. Please read only the odd numbered lines (1, 3, 5, and so on) for my true assessment of his ability......as follows:

Arthur Jones, my Administration Manager, can always be found hard at work at his desk. *Arthur works as a driven self-starter, without* **wasting company time talking to colleagues.** *Arthur never* thinks twice about helping his team mates and he always **finishes projects and assignments on time.** *Often Arthur takes extended* measures to complete his work, sometimes giving up **coffee breaks.** *Arthur is an individual who has absolutely no* vanity in spite of his high accomplishments and profound **knowledge in his field of administration.** *I firmly believe that Arthur can be* classed as an excellent, highly competent employee, the kind that cannot be **dispensed with. Consequently, I hereby recommend that Arthur be** promoted to executive management, and my proposal for this will be **executed as soon as possible.**

Thank you and best wishes,
Derek Hartley
Arthur Jones's Line Manager

The lesson here is, I suppose, always read between the lines!

Let us get back to recruitment. Once the boss of the human resources team has been selected, a vital responsibility is recruiting the right employees for the business. An assessment centre is now the popular method of finding new staff. Some companies run a series of these centres which are simply extended selection procedures, each lasting one or two days or sometimes longer. Generally this will be the first occasion for candidates to meet someone from the business they are interested in joining. Normally they are held either on employers' premises or in hotels and are considered by many organisations to be the fairest and most accurate method of selecting staff because a number of different selectors get to see candidates over a long period of time and have the chance to observe what they can do individually or in groups in various tests. The object of the assessment centre exercise is to test candidates, more often than not managers, for things like assertiveness, persuasive ability, communication effectiveness, planning and organising skills, self-confidence, control of stress and energy levels, decision-making capabilities, empathy with others, creativity, mental alertness and, last but not least, personal presence. Observers are looking at the whole person, but especially trying to identify experience, skills and personality. It is not an easy task and that is why it requires trained, capable and objective people to run the assessment process.

A typical assessment day would include a group exercise of sorts – a discussion perhaps on the subject of a deflating hot air balloon carrying ten people with the focus on who should be chucked overboard and in what order depending on characteristics and skills. Then it might be on to a task where pairs of candidates are challenged to build the tallest tower from old newspapers or the least wobbly bridge from Lego bricks. There may be numerical and verbal reasoning tests as well. Finally, conventional one-to-one interviews would seal the day. The first two phases would be watched by a group of assessor/observers who would meet after the candidates had left for the day to debate who had fared well and who would make it to the rejection pile. It was this end-of-day discussion that frustrated me because several assessors in various selection processes would let their egos get in the way of common sense. I often wonder how many candidates worthy of selection were ditched in the past because of a stubborn assessor's ego trip. Pressures of business, especially fast moving retail businesses, often steer recruiters into taking short cuts. In fact, it is probably better to cancel a recruitment centre rather than run it with a weak team of interviewers, assessors and observers. In reality though, very few HR managers would take this action. They would rather kid themselves that things will be fine and that it is better to muddle through than postpone. Any recruit that fails to perform in the job henceforward will be the one taken to task for weaknesses, rather than the HR manager pleading guilty to sloppy recruitment practices.

Here is my list of some of the important points to consider when running an assessment centre to recruit new employees:

- Prepare the assessment exercises and ensure they are relevant to the vacancies, easy to understand and as challenging as you feel appropriate to test the competencies of the candidates.

- Maintain high standards of selecting assessors, observers and interviewers. No compromises should be made to include incapable assessors.

- Communicate clearly with your chosen assessment team to ensure they understand the procedures, the assessment day schedules and the job roles to be filled, including an overview of the type and quality of the candidates invited to participate.

- Make sure that the assessment centre venue is suitable. It is sensible to rehearse the day with your team at the venue beforehand to ensure space is adequate, interview rooms are available, relaxation areas for candidates' breaks are clearly agreed and refreshments throughout the day are organised.

- Prepare all the materials for the event well in advance, including a master checklist, itinerary and exercise photocopies, furniture, stationery, candidate folders, interview scripts, etc.

- Start the assessment centre warmly and efficiently. Remember, the day is a two-way process so it is important to begin by giving the candidates an introduction to the company, the positions being recruited, what the day's arrangements will be and any relevant housekeeping or health and safety messages. Take time to break the ice, settle nerves and allow any questions for clarification.

- Give each candidate an opportunity to say a few words about themselves. It will help them to relax and is a useful way of creating a bond between the candidates themselves. It is also a technique that can reveal interesting hobbies and details to explore at the interview stage.

- Don't forget to provide feedback and guidance. It's important to remember that when you recruit, you are promoting your company, your attitude towards employees and yourselves as great examples of professional management. For both successful and unsuccessful candidates, the quality, honesty and clarity of your feedback should attract equal amounts of care and attention.

But I cannot stress enough, in all the games, simulations, tests, tasks and group discussions in an assessment centre, untrained and unprepared assessors and observers will weaken the process and increase the risk of incorrect selections. When all is said and done, when the mighty weight of HR intelligence and management science have influenced the outcome of a recruitment strategy, the proof of the decision-making is on the checkouts, behind the counters, on the service centre telephones and in all the other key positions that require interaction with customers. The evidence in stores and High Street shops and offices is that HR managers are letting companies down far too often by allowing too many unsuitable people into front-line customer service positions.

At this point I want to touch on the subject of customer service employee appearance and consider how important personal presentation is to retailing. Just as it is important to select with care, it is crucial that jobholders also look the part. The *Mail on Sunday* ran a report in 2009 about the high-class department store Harrods and the strict rules it applies to customer service staff. The newspaper had acquired internal staff guidelines, primarily focused on cosmetics, jewellery and perfume departments, including stipulations that female assistants should look timeless, sophisticated and elegant and are required to wear stiletto or kitten heels on the shop floor. Male members of staff are required to look smart, sophisticated and debonair, well-groomed with specific attention given to a restriction on beards and the length and width of sideburns. The rules on female and male dress and footwear standards are quite specific. Regulations on personal hygiene, breath freshness, manicured nails and personal jewellery are all part of the regime for female and male employees. The newspaper reported a Harrods spokesperson's confirmation that there are strict guidelines but they are not draconian. Some of the criteria reported for female employees:

- Timeless, sophisticated elegance
- Matching attire, clean and in good repair, no buckles, studs, logos, etc.
- Plain black, grey, navy or subtle pinstripe suits
- Full-length trousers and long-sleeve jackets
- Plain black, white or cream round neck or V-neck tops or fitted shirts
- Elegant, smart black leather shoes or boots, court-style with stiletto or kitten heels
- No open-toe footwear

Some of the criteria for male employees:

- Smart, sophisticated, debonair
- Plain black, grey, navy or subtle pinstripe suits without buckles, studs, etc.
- Shirts of a flattering fit and conservative ties
- Black smart footwear only, clean and in good repair
- No trainers, pumps or rubber soles
- No piercings, visible tattoos, mismatched jewellery or logos

There are other general rules about personal hygiene, including daily showering and hair washing, as well as breath freshness, and the wearing of name badges. I do not have any allegiance to Harrods but I think such a set of rules and regulations, if managed sensibly and with the customer in mind, is a very good, positive way to approach a retail business. The expected standard of appearance has to be clear or else anomalies set in as employees make their own decisions about fashion, jewellery and general body decoration. My career and life experience suggests that even a simplified adaptation of the Harrods rules would stand general retailing in good stead. It could be argued that they are being very fussy about dress standards and other aspects of personal appearance, but they have an image to uphold and that is how they choose to run things. Instead of paying lip service to a set of rules in an employee handbook as some retailers are prone to do, they are getting on with the job. They have the words and also the actions. As long as their staff members are aware of the rules before they accept a job, I cannot see any problem. In comparison, in High Streets and out-of-town stores, customer service is too erratic for comfort for all the reasons I have referred to before in this book, and the personal standards of a substantial number of customer servants are just as undisciplined. Harrods may have set the bar too high for most other retailers but they are being true to their respect for customers and I fail to see how anyone can argue with their intentions. Retailers at all levels of the socio-economic catchment grid should give serious consideration to devising their own rules.

If retailers want to sell, sell, sell and do it well, well, well (see Chapter 8), then great product choice and availability, operational efficiency and image protection as well as individual employee etiquette and appearance must be managed and controlled to the highest possible standards. If not, customers will be tempted to change allegiances and businesses will suffer as a result. Answer this question yourself, honestly – is it better to have a vacancy, with all the inconvenience of that, rather than put a badly chosen person in a crucial job? To state the obvious, get it right and the right people are in the right places doing the right things for customers. Get it wrong and the damage is done, not irreparable, but enough harm to interfere with the smooth running of the business. From my evidence of customer service and other operational aspects of business, there are an awful lot of poor standards out there, a major clue that HR is getting it wrong more than it should. One of the weakest links is, perhaps, the transient drifters seconded into important HR roles, the deficient career managers looking at each job as a stepping-stone rather than as a vocation in itself. The people in business deserve the very best management care and therefore, stating the obvious, the very, very best fully qualified and skilled people managers. The retail industry has come a long way but still has a long way to go.

Ssssssssh! "Retail Confidential" home truth alert:

Human Resources management in too many cases has allowed the theory of business science, psychometric testing and overblown recruitment shenanigans to cushion the need for businesses to be very careful and very selective when choosing recruitment teams. Amateurs in such a critically important process are dangerous. Recruitment campaigns can be cumbersome, time-consuming and long-winded – and, potentially, a waste of time and money if the erratic standard of employees let loose on the public is to be taken into account. If companies care enough about recruiting the right people, then how can they get it wrong on so many occasions? Why is there a disproportionate number of lemon-suckers out there in key service roles? Why do slick recruitment systems continue to offer flawed solutions?

8

HOW TO SELL, SELL, SELL AND DO IT WELL, WELL, WELL

I have in my possession a photocopy of song lyrics commissioned by British Home Stores, today's BHS, in the 1920s. It is called "See That We Sell It Today" and legend has it that every BHS shop had a piano and the staff would gather round each morning and sing this merry tune to enthuse them for the day's business. The song and the whole idea was a forerunner to the chanting and other motivational routines adopted by businesses all over the world to give employees a gee up. As I have indicated earlier when talking about workplace culture, it is debatable if singsongs, chants and other rituals actually contribute to increased sales or improved morale but, I suppose, it is a harmless activity with good intentions. The point is that a retailer without sales is like a pub with no beer – pointless and doomed. So, sometimes retailers have to dip into a little bit of show business to boost the coffers and employees' energy levels. Retailing is a simple business often strangled by complications, especially in the good times. But when customers are few and sales are in decline, somehow the retailer's instinct seems to revert to the basics of shops, shoppers, selling and service. It seems to be a natural inbred reaction. The complications, thankfully, seem take a back seat. Fighting to survive concentrates the mind. There are so many external factors affecting business that it is easy to become distracted away from the things that really matter. My favourite quotation of all time is from the US politician Donald Rumsfeld on global matters, but I think it can refer to anything, particularly when analysing crises and hand-wringing our way through subsequent soul-searching. He said: "There are known knowns. These are things we know that we know. There are known unknowns. That is to say, there are things that we know we don't know. But there are also unknown unknowns. There are things we don't know we don't know." It is worth bearing that in mind, if you can be bothered with the embroidered language, that in there somewhere is an important message. I draw from it the lesson that dealing with the things we know is far more productive than obsessing with things that we do not know, or things that are well out of our control. If we stick to our knitting, we will get a jumper rather than a long scarf. My Granny was a philosopher too.

Much of this book is being written in 2009 and all around us, major retail brand names are disappearing faster than ice cubes in a furnace. The biggest High Street casualty so far has been Woolworths, but the numbers grow, specifically with independent retailers. Some medium-sized towns in the UK are seeing more and more chipboard window covers and "closing down" signs. Surviving retailers are in the process of considering or actually cutting jobs by thousands. It is a credit-crunchingly grim time. But retailing is a tough business run, by and large, by people ready, willing and able to make tough decisions. As the soul guru Billy Ocean told us, "When the going gets tough, the tough get going." One option, or at least a tandem measure with other actions, is for retailers to simply cut costs. But the primary action for the survival of the retail fittest is to find ways to boost sales. When an economy starts stalling and spluttering, streetwise, savvy business people take action instinctively, and activating selling energy is essential for the blood flow in the veins of this industry. The object of the exercise of any retail store operation is to find ways to get customers into the shops. Marketing boffins call this footfall and it is marketeers that play a significant role in trying to come up with sexy, sassy ways to attract the general public with its wallets and purses, through the doors.

Marketing slogans are crucial, of course, to win customers by using sophisticated brain washing, luring and manipulating people into remembering and trusting companies. Here is a reminder of some slogans and hooks to influence, educate, flatter, tantalise, seduce and reel us into making sales:

- Every Little Helps *(Tesco)*
- Pocket The Difference *(Asda)*
- Save Money, Live Better *(Wal-Mart)*
- Expect More, Pay Less *(Target Stores)*
- Touching Lives, Improving Life *(Procter & Gamble)*
- That Was Easy *(Staples)*
- Committed To People, Committed To The Future *(Toyota)*
- Connecting People *(Nokia)*
- Just Do It *(Nike)*
- Good Food, Good Life *(Nestle)*

Slogans, warm and cuddly as they are meant to be, can seep into our consuming souls and infiltrate our thoughts like a market-hating meerkat, for example. Simples! Ask the older generation to deny believing that a chocolate bar made by Mars can help you work, rest and play. They will not be able to disown the memory. It is debatable, of course, that a cocoa-infused confection has such powers but we cannot forget it as a piece of product propaganda. It works and companies know it. A colleague of mine from my trainee manager days said that the best way to get customers into the shop was to have a big sign outside with a message in large letters saying "We are giving away money today", and in tiny letters at the bottom the words "it's called your change." I predicted a riot but he was only half-joking. However, beyond the slogans, there is much to ponder and much to explore. In these heady days of world-wide web technology, of online shopping, Facebook, Twitter, blogs and so on, the store wars battlefield has expanded from High Street to hi-tech. The whole business of retailing has become very, very personal, with frightening quantities of detailed information about us all building up on company databases. We think they are being chummy by wanting us to be their friends but all they really want is our dosh. We are targets and they are commercial marksmen. It is a fascinating subject but I will leave cyber retailing for another time. The truth is that as long as the bricks and mortar of physical retail buildings exist, good old-fashioned techniques are necessary to win customers, draw them in through the doors to buy, buy, buy. In addition, despite technology's relentless grip on the virtual world, there is enough to contend with anyway in retailing's real world on terra firma. Just consider all the ways people are trying to get a share of your spending money. Apart from big names in High Street and out-of-town outlets, there are charity shops, second-hand shops, car boot sales, mobile shops, airport shops, railway station shops, market stalls, yard sales and Ann Summers and Tupperware parties in people's houses. It is a jungle out there and the strong, energetic and resourceful will survive, while the weak fade away.

The tried and tested theory of the marketing mix – product, price, place, promotion – combines essential ingredients to implement for commercial success. It allows as much flexibility as necessary with each ingredient to accommodate changes in a company's development, the types of products and services on sale, the strength of competitors, the fickleness of customers and external factors, particularly things that affect the economy and specifically the amount of disposable income available to spenders. To the four Ps – product, price, place, promotion – I would add, of course, another P – people. I have covered a number of aspects of people already because, obvious as it sounds, in retailing it is always important to combine physical buildings, fixtures and fittings, with flesh and blood. I always remember Asda's Allan Leighton telling us at a conference that the only option for a company in people terms was to have leaders and followers. He said, "If you are a leader, then lead. If you are a follower, then follow. If you have any problems with either of these two roles, then leave." His point was stark, of course, but clear and correct. Retailing is more and more like a series of military campaigns and it needs decisive generals as well as obedient troops.

In retailing, the two main headline challenges are:

- To have the right products at the right price in the right place at the right time
- To have the right people in the right places at the right time

Three key areas of focus are:

- Customers

- Inventory
- Staffing

The challenges and areas of focus must be clearly understood even before opening the front doors of the shop. If the products are not in demand, the offer will struggle. If the wrong people are serving, the business's reputation will decline rapidly. Taking time to manage the two challenges and focus areas thoroughly and properly will sort the winning wheat from the losing chaff amongst retailers. Assuming the agenda has been met, successful retailing then relies on a degree of science applied practically and sensibly. The concept of category management is an important planning tool and invites intelligent thinking on the following:

- Understanding why customers decide where to shop and where not to shop and devising strategies to continue to attract the loyal consumers and to win over the non-believers

- Considering ways to seduce customers into and then around the shop, planning the most lucrative "customer path" route through aisles and offers

- Devoting as much resource as possible to comprehending evolving customer behaviour, including their allegiances to causes (environment, wildlife, healthy eating, healthy living, etc.) and the business benefit from following trends, tuning into the popular ideas of the day and jumping on as many beneficial bandwagons as necessary.

A supermarket manager who wished to remain anonymous told me that modern day shop management in big box store food retailing is much more pressurised than ever before and the amount of checking and auditing on stock availability has never been more intense – and threatening. He told me that if an audit sequence shows a below-par product availability score then the "three strikes and you're out" rule kicks in. When it comes to people losing their jobs, you realise the significance of some aspects of present-day retailing. Supermarkets have become war zone participants, constantly fighting rivals, and managers who are either deemed not competent enough or, dare I say, too old and too expensive, are prone to get the boot. The selling game has always been serious but a certain savagery has crept in, even with all the fine and fancy talk of coaching and mentoring better performances from people. Another manager quipped that it would be easier to swim naked through a sea of razor blades than manage a food store, for all sorts of internal and external reasons. The point I am making is that retailing in certain sectors and for certain job roles is not for the faint-hearted. But managers also complain that they are sometimes at the mercy of too dictatorial bosses or too unreceptive employees. Whatever opinions and complaints are swilling around nowadays, a food store without food when people want it is no good to anyone. So it is no wonder that availability of stock commands so much time, technology and attention. A former Asda director used to say: "It's only value if it's there." He was and is right, of course, but there is so much more to retailing than this one, albeit, important aspect, although sales and selling are the highest priorities.

I spent eighteen months touring the UK as a retail specialist to try to find ways to help and support motorcycle clothing shops to sell more and operate better. It was a tough challenge, not least because most of the shops involved were independently owned and final decisions on proposed changes rested with the owners themselves. Some of the owners were very receptive to "fresh eyes", others were ambivalent or choosy about which pieces of advice to accept and which to discard, and a few owners could not be bothered to listen or experiment, preferring to believe in their own abilities to move their businesses forward. Inevitably, the ideas that cost nothing were generally popular and the suggestions requiring some investment were subjects for much debate and compromise. I would not blame any of the retailers for their particular stances but I would criticise a few for being stubborn and short-sighted in their analysis of present requirements for future success. Retailing relies on a degree of vision, of risk-taking and sometimes people are happy to be cosy in their comfort world. It is not a blame game, more a choice. But the reason I choose this period in my retail career to illustrate some of the methodology I use when tackling retail challenges is because it involves small shops, generally speaking – distinctly different environments entirely from the gigantic palaces run by the major operators. The settings for small shops are, by definition and design, more intimate, with compact sales floor space and small teams to run the business. I always began my observations outside in the street or the mall walkway to get first impressions, before entering the shops to have a look around. This is the broad checklist I used:

EXTERIOR:
- Fascia clean and in good order
- Windows clean and displays attractive
- Displayed information relevant and accurate
- Outside area clean and free of litter
- Front door easy to open (you'd be surprised!)

INTERIOR
- Immediate entrance clutter-free and clean
- Shop team available and well-groomed
- Walls, ceiling, lighting, fixtures and fittings in good condition
- Fair balance between display space and customer browsing space
- Signage and merchandise well presented

This brief list requires good powers of absorbing details at a glance. As I looked I would be asking myself simple but effective questions like these:

- Is the shop clean or dirty?
- Is it full or empty?
- Is it tidy or untidy?
- Is it attractive to customers or repulsive?
- Is it welcoming or unwelcoming?"

Thankfully, some shop teams took my advice about the importance of daily routines on board and improved their ways of working and tidied up their shops. Others had a half-hearted go at it but drifted back into their lazy ways, assuming that this stuff is not as important as I was trying to make it sound. We are well enough into this book for me to dig out the old chestnut and confirm that retail is definitely about detail, although in a lot of shops the penny has not dropped. As a customer myself, I would cite the example of most sports shops and how difficult they make it for customers to shop. I refuse to go into them because they get so much of these basic disciplines wrong, especially the ratio of selling pace to customer space.

In my experience, it is nearly impossible to stand and browse in a sporting goods store because so many fixtures are crammed in. The proportion of merchandised space to customer space is all skewed and wrong. Stand and look at a rack of merchandise for a few moments and count how many times you have to move out of the way to let other people through. It is frustrating, annoying and, frankly, it loses sales because no serious shopper likes to be shuffled and nudged out of the way while considering making a buying decision. All through my career, I have heard the glib phrase "less is more" and I have not always understood it. But when it comes to sports shops in particular and store layouts generally, I know exactly what it means – less fixtures and more legroom for customers. It is a simple truth in an unnecessarily complicated world, that uncluttered focus on customers reaps rewards in the till. Sales are possible, of course, even if customer service is poor and walk-round space limited but the lifespan of a business would be curtailed, no doubt. Sales and great service spawn loyalty, repeat business and new clientele. So "see that we sell it today" continues to be a great mantra after all these years even if the simplicity of the lyrics has been replaced with modern complications of managing finances, employees, customers, space, stock, productivity and compliance with the law. Here is a list to help anyone thinking about mounting a retail improvement campaign. It is an analytical series of questions to help get to the heart of your business and your people:

- What do we do now? (Clarify what your business is all about)
- How do we do it? (Look at the way things are done. Are you satisfied?)
- When do we do it? (Consider opening hours and customer convenience)

- Where do we do it? (Be aware of your location and its strengths and weaknesses)
- Who does it? (Happy with your team?)
- What else could you do to improve the business? (Consider new products and services)
- How else could the business prosper? (Are there other marketing opportunities?)
- When is the business at its strongest and weakest? (Look at your sales trends)
- Where else could make a difference? (Is your location right for your business?)
- Who else could make a difference? (Are the individuals in the team the right people?)

There are many ways to look at retail sales performance, internally and externally. Looking inwards, to the people in your business, can expose a huge treasure chest of ideas to boost transactions. Here are some questions to ask your employees every three months or so:

- What is your idea to improve the shop, customer service, team morale and the business?
- What is the financial benefit of each of your four ideas?
- What is the degree of difficulty in implementing your four ideas?
- What is the estimated cost of each of your for ideas?
- What is the first step in implementing each of your four ideas?

I like to start with the premise that the people who do a particular job know best how that job should be done, what makes it difficult to do at times and what would make the job easier to do. Team involvement in everything the business is about can be a massive strength, from how things are done to how people look and behave. I have covered some ground already talking about hiring and managing the right employees, but I think it is worth emphasising some of the points again when considering sales and selling. It is possible to sell using inanimate vending machines of course, but people still count in most retailing businesses, so consider the following section carefully. Here are some pointers when assessing the characteristics of superb customer servants, remembering in general that most of us hate the hard sell but love great service. Look for these attributes as part of your sales and selling strategy:

- Do they look the part in their smart appearance and polite manner?
- Do they look as if they are happy to be in a serving role?
- Do they greet customers every time?
- Do they have a natural, friendly demeanour?
- Do they have the aptitude and interest to absorb and relay product knowledge?
- Do they have the ability and patience to listen?
- Do they use customer contact opportunities to suggest extra items?
- Do they always thank customers, regardless of a sale or not?
- Do they maintain their respect for customers on and off the job?
- Do they have the boss's complete confidence in their important role as customer servants?

Once the best people are in place and assuming the right stock is in the stores at the right levels to satisfy demand, here are some aspects of sales promotion to get you thinking about how to sell more:

- Create in-store displays with maximum impact in prime locations
- Erect special fixtures and display stands to attract interest
- Use strong signage (banners, posters, etc.) to draw attention and shout the offers
- Highlight buy-one-get-one-free, three-for-two, multi-save, multi-buy promotions
- Consider distinctive packaging or on-pack stickers to highlight offers
- Design leaflets, catalogues, tip sheets, etc., to educate and inform

- Install audio-visual support to illustrate and entertain
- Organise special event evenings and competitions
- Plan for exciting demonstration and sampling areas
- Advertise as much as you can afford

A former colleague of mine said once that he enjoyed his job so much that he was embarrassed to accept his salary every month. He said that selling was an easy way to earn a living and leading people was a privilege, so why should his conscience allow him to take money for it. I agreed with him about the latter notion regarding people but I told him, rather rudely I concede, that he was a pillock about selling being easy, and doubly so for being guilty about his wages. It was never easy but it is certainly harder physical work than ever either in manhandling pallets of product or refining sales patter with customers. When you cut to the chase, retailing is really only about selling and everything else including service, administration, morale and obeying the law pales into lower positions on the priority ladder. Many will argue about this notion but the truth is out there. I have been ordered to make cuts, I have made cuts independently, I have cut the corners and I have the scars and bruises to back it up.

Ssssssssh! "Retail Confidential" home truth alert:

Retailers will do almost anything to sell stuff. They will embrace the marketing mix in theory at least and gather the requisite amount of employees of mixed ability together to get the job done. But, most of the time, they are inclined or forced by circumstances to cut corners with distribution and staff quality either through economic or hasty decision- making or due to influences outside their control, trying to get away with lapses and mistakes in availability and service as much as they can. Some of the theories of retailing are a Grand Canyon apart from their implementation and practice and every now and again, to the detriment of customer service and staff morale, the four Ps of the marketing mix and the one P for people are joined by P for Panic, P for Pandemonium and P for Phew-I-Think-We-Got-Away-With-It!

9

HOW A WEEK CAN BE A LIFETIME FOR A SUPERMARKET MANAGER

The longest week of my retail life was at Christmas a few years ago. I was managing a food and non-food superstore in the Midlands. The strategy for this most important season had been set a few months before at a Christmas conference where store general managers were reminded of the fact that 40% of the year's sales depended on the October to December period. We were informed that product availability, especially fresh food, would be second to none, more than ample to meet demand. This was big business for fresh turkeys, vegetables, hams, meat, pork pies, dips, salads, cheeses and all the rest of it, so to miss out on sales by not getting the supply and distribution chains right would be close to disaster for the profit and loss account. But what happened in the course of the big week leading up to Christmas was challenging, frightening and, in some ways, dangerous.

The buyers had bought enormous quantities of fresh food. The directors had signed off the plan. The store managers had to manage at best and cope at worst with increased deliveries of pallets and pallets and pallets of fresh food, before more and more pallets arrived. The rules of fresh food handling dictated that we had to receive the delivery and have it checked and refrigerated in chilled conditions within an hour at most, but twenty minutes was the ideal target. Even Tom Cruise would have found that mission impossible. But, and if ever a subject deserved to be in a book called "Retail Confidential", I can reveal that huge quantities of fresh food did not see refrigeration storage for days. Luckily, the weather was on our side. Outside in the warehouse yard, it was bitterly cold and so, I suppose, by default, we complied with chilled conditions. But the fact of the matter was that the amount of food sent to us, predetermined by buyers and merchandisers, far outweighed our storage capacity on the premises. On our daily Christmas conference call, store managers voiced concern about the avalanche of food arriving several times each day. On one of the calls, the Chief Executive of the company brushed our concerns aside and told us that our top priority this Christmas was to maintain availability of all fresh food products to closing time on Christmas Eve. He seemed unconcerned about the mountains of food being stored in supermarket yards for upwards of forty-eight hours. The general public had no idea. All across the UK, delivery areas of supermarkets were choked full of product that belonged in properly refrigerated storage. We had to manage the situation as best we could and we did, with flying colours, if flying by the seat of our pants was a legitimate way of working. We got away with it because of the weather but it taught me a few lessons about sales pressure and the ability of some senior people in retailing to turn a blind eye to practical problems, preferring to concentrate on the balance sheet above and beyond customer safety and care sometimes.

But, apart from odd weeks like that, most weeks for a retail store manager are a mixture of people interaction, dull routines and lots and lots of administration. It is a role where job status is emphasised by the job title but in practice the role can be an alien brew of dynamism and drudgery. I remember a visit to one of my stores from a Venezuelan businessman and he told me that in his country, I would be treated like royalty because a management position in retailing was regarded as a very high status job. He also said that I would need a gun as a highly-paid manager was a great target for kidnappers. So I went from rosy-cheeked pride to ashen horror in a matter of seconds and discarded his implied compliment, returning my ego to ground level. In fact, or at least in my experienced opinion, retail managers are seen to be less important than they used to be. The days, and I assure you there were such days, when a store manager could spend all his (for it once was a totally male-dominated position) time in his office selecting booze from his alcohol cabinet and drinking himself silly are well and truly over. When I took over as general manager at a wholesale warehouse in Liverpool, I was told that I had just missed the drinks cabinet being removed from the premises. It seems unbelievable now but booze was seen as a perk and daytime drinking for some executives in retailing and wholesaling was accepted.

In these more sober times, I investigated how current supermarket managers define their week. In the good old bad old days, it was a simpler arrangement of five days out of six (for Sunday, my child, was a day of rest) and between 9.00am and 6.00pm. Today, most supermarkets are operating twenty four hours a day across seven days and smaller units have variations on extended hours and late night shopping. The management shift pattern has changed completely. A store manager, broadly speaking, is expected to work five days out of seven, with regular Saturday and Sunday attendance inherent in their responsibilities. Day, twilight and night shifts require management presence and most large companies stipulate that the store manager should operate within a pattern of work taking in all shifts over a month. Several times a year, supermarket managers are now expected to spend two weeks or more working through the night. It is debatable whether all this shift changing is actually a good thing, but there is a climate of enforced fairness in business, as indeed there is in politics. The status formerly afforded to "the boss" has been eroded by bureaucracy, in my opinion, and the gaffer is as much on the supermarket treadmill as anybody.

But, to avoid my drift into diatribe, here is my recollection of seven days in the life of a typical supermarket manager. It is routine, not all bad, not all dull but leaning sometimes in the direction of mundanity. Hell, we're supermarket managers, not adventure seekers.

Sunday:

Walk around the store, talk to people, fix anything that can be fixed as we go, make notes of stuff to be attended to later. Have coffee, a bite to eat, more coffee and go home.

Monday:

Walk around the store, talk to people, fix anything that can be fixed as we go, make notes of stuff to be attended to later. Have coffee, a bite to eat, more coffee and go home.

Tuesday:

Walk around the store, talk to people, fix anything that can be fixed as we go, make notes of stuff to be attended to later. Have coffee, a bite to eat, more coffee and go home.

Wednesday:

Walk around the store, talk to people, fix anything that can be fixed as we go, make notes of stuff to be attended to later. Have coffee, a bite to eat, more coffee and go home.

Thursday:

Walk around the store, talk to people, fix anything that can be fixed as we go, make notes of stuff to be attended to later. Have coffee, a bite to eat, more coffee and go home.

Friday:

Walk around the store, talk to people, fix anything that can be fixed as we go, make notes of stuff to be attended to later. Have coffee, a bite to eat, more coffee and go home.

Saturday:

Walk around the store, talk to people, fix anything that can be fixed as we go, make notes of stuff to be attended to later. Have coffee, a bite to eat, more coffee and go home.

I know I am being simplistic and facetious, but the core of my illustration is true. Even reading the previous few lines should give you a sense of tedium and, believe me, retailing is full of tedium. A week is a long time in the business and sometimes it is up to you to create your own interests and excitements. One of the best ways I and many of my colleagues have found over the years is our own telephone gossip when we could chew the fat and criticise the business and our bosses, make jokes about the inefficiencies and foibles of our masters. It was and hopefully still is one of the joys of retail management to hide yourself away and natter on for an hour or so with another management soulmate about all the trouble and strife in the business.

Every now and again the daily and weekly agenda would be broken up with meetings, disciplinary matters, seasonal layout changes, senior management visits and all sorts of other distractions involving shoplifters or customer complaints. If I tell you that I once had to devote the best part of four days to assess all the information and decide upon an alleged staff theft incident involving a can of Coca Cola, then you might understand how this simple business of selling can be screwed up in an instant. If I relate to you the hours and hours I had to devote to a customer complaint involving our landscape gardeners who had mistakenly cut down twenty feet of hedge belonging to an irate neighbour, then you might grasp an inkling of some of the nonsense we have to deal with. If I describe to you the substantial amount of time I spent on the telephone and in person with a resident of a street three miles away from my store about his rage at how one of our carrier bags had managed to lodge itself in his apple tree, I hope I can squeeze a droplet of understanding that I really would love to spend my time selling but other stuff gets in the way. If I tell you that when I worked as general manager in a hypermaket in the Midlands, there was not a day when I wasn't more than ten steps into the building before someone would offload a problem with blocked drains, leaking roof, broken bakery equipment, high absenteeism on the night shift shelf filling team or in one exciting case, a suspected large black rodent in the warehouse, then maybe, just maybe, you will get some comprehension about the real life of a store manager.

We want to sell, we love to sell, we want to be amongst our teams, we love action and enjoy the purist form of retailing – selling and having fun doing it. But it is not often as easy as it sounds. In my early days in BHS, my boss had a sign on the wall behind his desk. It read: "What a wonderful day. Now, watch some clown mess it up." How true. How true. On most days, I would arrive with a plan in my head for the ten hours ahead but within minutes the plan was consigned to the bin. So, whilst I am an advocate of organisation, planning and routine to an extent, I am enough of a realist to know that it is wise to have as loose a plan as possible because that is the way active retailing works.

Finally, in this section, I want to relate to you a little tale of experience. A young manager told me that he had a bad memory and that he felt it would hinder his career. He said there was so much to do in retailing that he had not the confidence to remember all the important stuff, and that in time he would feel undermined and inadequate as he progressed his career. I told him that in this simple world of complications and distractions he had not been burdened with a bad memory, and I would prove it to him. "In your daily working life," I began, "you will remember to do at least five things. You will arrive at work, have your coffee, have your lunch, have your afternoon tea and go home. There you are, five things you will not forget to do." He looked at me either like a disciple in awe of a god or a whimpering newborn kitten craving a saucer of milk. He uttered the one word a guru does not want to hear from a student. "Eh?" I believed I had proven that he did not have a bad memory and he had convinced himself that I was nuts. Such is business life. Such is the wafer-thin bond between boss and employee. A week is a long time for a supermarket manager and sometimes even five minutes can be a lifetime.

SUMMARY OF PART ONE

Throughout this book I have tried to give you a flavour of retailing from my perspective, some true stories, some opinions and a lot of suggestions. On balance, after such a long career, I love retailing with all its imperfections, rather like a jeweller loves a flawed diamond. I hope I have explained my credentials clearly enough, with a little help from Butch and Sundance, who, come to think about it would be two ideal supermarket managers in the all-guns-blazing, fast-moving world of consumer goods. ("Think you used enough planograms there, Butch?") I discussed the complicated way we run such a simple and straightforward business. It beggars belief that retailing has become the cryptic crossword puzzle rather than the coffee-time teaser. I trawled through the wild and wacky worlds of company cultures and tried to illustrate the shallowness of a lot of the slogans and gimmicks, even though it seems to work in some businesses. You accompanied me on a journey through customer service and we heard about some of the good, bad and ugly things that happen out there. We should all wish a plague on the "lemon-suckers" and the people who hire them. I had a little fun with some true customer complaints and I still shudder at the price I paid out for those two avocado pears. I explained about people and how too many retailers get it wrong when recruiting staff. It is astonishing. I covered some aspects of selling and its inherent pressures and how difficult it can be sometimes, especially with the many distractions that eat up valuable time and sap the spirit.

If you are a retail veteran or if you are new to the industry, I hope you recognise or absorb some of the reality that I have been trying to share. If you think I am way off the mark or too critical or too flippant, then write your version. This is how I see it. Thank you for reading, so far, and please call again.

PART TWO:
RETAIL OPERATIONS DIGEST OF
HELPFUL LISTS AND HANDY HINTS

CONTENTS:

LESSONS FROM MY CAREER
10 lessons I learned from BHS
10 lessons I learned from Alfred Dunhill Ltd
10 lessons I learned from the Bolton Abbey Estate
10 lessons I learned from Makro
10 lessons I learned from Asda/Wal-Mart
10 questions retail people should ask and say "yes" to

LESSONS ABOUT CUSTOMERS
10 customer types I encountered over the years
10 lessons about retailers' negative attitudes to customers
10 ways to get customers to trust you
10 things a retailer wants a loyal customer to remember
10 essential ingredients of face-to-face customer service
10 basic ways retailers can impress customers

LESSONS ON IMPROVING RETAIL BUSINESS PERFORMANCE
10 retail ingredients to understand and manage
10 things to consider for the best shop experience
10 factors in a winning strategy
10 ways to win business
10 ways to improve retail sales

LESSONS ABOUT GETTING THE BEST OUT OF INDIVIDUALS   AND TEAMS
10 ways to get things done
10 lessons about listening
10 ways to nurture team involvement
10 time management tips
10 ways to get feedback if you really want some
10 things to stop you worrying
10 alarm bells suggesting you are unhappy at work
10 things to ponder when in a predicament

LESSONS FROM THE WORLD AROUND US
10 business-related quotations
10 Beatles songs to prompt you into action
10 Bob Dylan songs to make you think
10 Rolling Stones songs for job satisfaction
10 commandments adapted for business
10 proverbs offering good old-fashioned wisdom
10 mottoes to inspire

INTRODUCTION

In my long career, I have enjoyed reading and learning about retailing. I have lost count of the number of weighty books I have ploughed through, the amount of business magazines I have combed and the financial pages of newspapers I have glanced at. My ears have almost exploded and my brain liquefied as I listened to long lectures and tedious training presentations on business improvement in years gone by. Over time, I developed a penchant for succinct lists, bullet points, handy hints, top tips and prompts to stimulate my imagination, to help me resolve problems and to guide me through the sometimes wild and whacky world of retailing. This section contains a series of such lists, a digest for you to dip into whenever you need some help. Some of the lists are in here for fun because fun should be part of any job description. Let me start by reminding you of the things I like and dislike about business. Writing down my preferences helps me to appreciate the satisfying aspects of work and the challenges of the downside. As I have declared at the beginning of the book, the ten things I love about business are interaction with people, opportunities to hone communication skills; the challenge of scaling the heights of customer satisfaction; opportunities to stimulate ideas; challenging team projects; unselfishness from great teamwork; opportunities to develop the skill of humour; competitiveness; pace, cohesion in adversity and celebration of success, including financial rewards. The ten things I hate about business are apathetic leadership, poor communication, bad planning, erratic organisation, lousy manners, boring meetings, untidy workspaces, declining morale, mischief-makers and gossips. Now, use these lists but do yourself an extra favour and write your own lists. It is a useful exercise. Here are mine. One or two you will recognise from the first part of the book. The rest are new.

1. LESSONS FROM MY CAREER

10 LESSONS I LEARNED FROM BHS

1. The importance of organising time
2. Routines of morning and evening department inspections
3. Identifying personal mentors and role models
4. A deep respect for people
5. The critical nature of teamworking
6. The dangers of big-headedness
7. How to deal with the unexpected
8. A "can do" attitude
9. The place for fun in business
10. Nurturing a genuine love for retailing

10 LESSONS I LEARNED FROM ALFRED DUNHILL LTD

1. To be more organised
2. To work more efficiently from a distance
3. To be a more articulate speaker
4. To develop a voice with personality
5. To understand the need for a trustworthy tone
6. To listen actively
7. To think on my feet
8. To communicate progress frequently
9. To follow-through on details
10. To appreciate the support team around me

10 LESSONS I LEARNED FROM THE BOLTON ABBEY ESTATE

1. To relish challenges out of my comfort zone
2. To take time to familiarise myself with individuals
3. To hone my presentation skills
4. To adapt my body language and voice to individual needs
5. To expect, endure and recover quickly from setbacks
6. To stick to my professional principles
7. To work at displaying a transparent persona
8. To understand that not all arguments can be won by me
9. To accept constructive criticism
10. To enjoy success and learn from failure

10 LESSONS I LEARNED FROM MAKRO

1. The enormous responsibility and privilege of leading a large team of people
2. The intensity of business-to-business challenges in cash and carry wholesaling
3. The competitive nature of local community marketing
4. The pleasure and pain of almost total autonomy to run the business
5. The development of trusting customer relationships
6. The ability to think and decide quickly to deal with the unexpected
7. The benefits of open and honest communication with everyone
8. The ways to deal with the after effects of ram raiding (three times!)
9. The trauma for everyone involved in an Industrial Tribunal (first time)
10. The fact that store management in not a solo endeavour

10 LESSONS I LEARNED FROM ASDA/WAL-MART

1. The importance of a defined mission statement for clarity of direction
2. The necessity of a moral compass in a set of company values
3. The essential involvement of all employees in contributing ideas and taking responsibility
4. The benefits to personal efficiency of disciplines and routines
5. The fact that the challenges of managing workplace morale never end
6. The clarity of focus on customer care
7. The need to coach and mentor talent for future business survival
8. The moral duty to challenge upwards, regardless of personal risk
9. The significance of rewarding success
10. The fickleness of individuals in teams

10 QUESTIONS RETAIL PEOPLE SHOULD ASK AND SAY "YES" TO

1. Do I like selling?
2. Do I enjoy shops and shopping?
3. Do I like people?
4. Do I like teamworking?
5. Do I like motivating and being motivated?
6. Do I embrace the idea of doing a little more that my job description?
7. Do I like being managed?
8. Do I like to learn and keep learning?
9. Do I enjoy merchandising and working to high standards?
10. Do I see a great personal future in retailing?

2. LESSONS ABOUT CUSTOMERS

10 CUSTOMER TYPES I ENCOUNTERED OVER THE YEARS

1. **The Sprinter** – the one that comes in, chooses, buys and leaves without catching a breath
2. **The Browser** – the one that seems to be killing time but just might part with their money
3. **The Decisive Buyer** – the one that knows exactly what they want, mind already made up
4. **The Ditherer** – the one that needs equal measures of attention and product knowledge
5. **The Silent Type** – the one that chooses to be uncommunicative
6. **The Talker** – the one that loves to chat and chat and, er, chat
7. **The Distrusting Customer** – the one that reckons retailers are disreputable
8. **The Know-all** – the one that cannot be told anything new
9. **The Obnoxious Kind** – the one that is always out for confrontation
10. **The Sweetheart** – the one that is an absolute joy to serve because they are no trouble

10 LESSONS ABOUT RETAILERS' NEGATIVE ATTITUDES TO CUSTOMERS

1. That we (retailers) can be snobbish in our superiority about what customers really want
2. That we can bluff customers into believing that their feedback makes a difference
3. That we are much more inconsistent in our delivery of service than we care to admit
4. That we see customers more as money machines than human beings
5. That we see customers as statistics first to create trends, graphs and charts
6. That we make decisions more for balance sheet reasons than customer service
7. That insults and disrespectful comments about customers are commonplace in retailing
8. That customers are not always right even though we tell them they are
9. That complaining customers will receive disproportionately more goodwill gestures
10. That we are a hybrid of hypocrisy and hubris when it comes to customer behaviour

10 WAYS TO GET CUSTOMERS TO TRUST YOU

1. Remember customers are flesh and blood like you
2. Consult with them frequently to understand their needs
3. Be crystal clear as to what you do and what you guarantee
4. Think about transactions as steps in building a positive relationship
5. Never lie and never over-promise
6. Always return telephone calls and answer mail promptly
7. Answer customers' questions – you're in business not politics
8. Apologise when necessary and go over the top to make things right
9. Surprise your customers with little rewards throughout the year
10. Ensure your team's commitment to the highest standards of customer care

10 THINGS A RETAILER WANTS A LOYAL CUSTOMER TO REMEMBER

1. **Familiarity** – a credible retailer you know or become aware of via word of mouth
2. **Reliability** – a retailer to count on above all the others most of the time
3. **Customer service** – knowing that service will be always be sincere and efficient
4. **Quality** – value for money in action
5. **Consistency** – over time, a retailer that maintains very high standards
6. **Guarantee** – secure in the knowledge that the retailer is safe to do business with
7. **Value** – confidence that your money will be well spent
8. **Efficiency** – a retailer that realises a customer's time is important too
9. **Personality** – a retailer with a genuine smile on its face
10. **Friendliness** – the simple feeling that the shop staff like and respect you

10 ESSENTIAL INGREDIENTS OF FACE-TO-FACE CUSTOMER SERVICE

1. Hello, good morning or some other warm, sincere greeting
2. Attention fully given to the person you are serving to let them know they are special
3. Please, thank you and all the other expressions of sincerely delivered good manners
4. Put on a genuine smile as part of your uniform
5. You are there to serve, so accept it and look (be) happy doing your job
6. Seek to interact with customers if they are happy to chat while you work
7. Make every effort to let customers know you are happy to help in any way
8. "I will be the best customer servant ever today," should be your daily mantra
9. Let customers know you like what you do through your body language and attitude
10. Ensure you say goodbye to customers with a warm parting comment

10 BASIC WAYS RETAILERS CAN IMPRESS CUSTOMERS

1. Shop fascia clean and in good order
2. Windows clean and displays attractive
3. Displayed information relevant and accurate
4. Outside area clean and free of litter
5. Front door easy to open (you'd be surprised!)
6. Immediate entrance clutter-free and clean
7. Shop team available and of smart appearance
8. Walls, ceiling, lighting, fixtures and fittings in good condition
9. Fair balance between display space and customer browsing space
10. Signage and merchandise well presented

3. LESSONS ABOUT IMPROVING RETAIL BUSINESS PERFORMANCE

10 RETAIL INGREDIENTS TO UNDERSTAND AND MANAGE

1. Customer types you are aiming to attract – who are they and what do they want?
2. Location and catchment area – where your customers come from?
3. The shop – is it accessible and easy for customers to circulate, browse and buy?
4. Employees – try to reflect your local area's population, if possible
5. Local community groups, schools, charities, etc – get involved and boost your integrity
6. Local authorities – know who you are dealing with in areas of due diligence
7. Local press – it's great for updating yourself on events and for publishing press releases
8. Competitors' activity – learn what they do well and what they do badly, and act on it
9. Embrace change to suit local requirements
10. Find ways for your shop to become indispensible to the catchment area

10 THINGS TO CONSIDER FOR THE BEST SHOP EXPERIENCE

1. Shop image as portrayed on the front fascia – what are you saying to customers?
2. Shop atmosphere – customers have great radar about what feels right and wrong
3. Shop design – colour scheme, lighting, etc can turn on or turn off
4. Shop layout – how fixtures, signs, displays, etc., are placed and arranged counts
5. Shop signage – quality and quantity of signs need careful consideration to avoid clutter
6. Shop selling space versus customer space requires due regard
7. Shop merchandise should be available to meet demand and be presented attractively
8. Shop service people should be perfect in appearance and etiquette
9. Shop opening and closing times should reflect customer demands
10. Shop managers should interact as much as is humanly possible with staff and customers

10 FACTORS IN A WINNING STRATEGY

1. Look at ways to continuously improve efficiency throughout the business
2. Keep driving revenue, cash flow and cost controls
3. Know what you are doing, why you are doing it and vow to keep operations simple
4. Do unto others as you would like them to do unto you – i.e. behave well always
5. Involve all your employees in business improvements and reward individual success
6. Use facts and logic when making business decisions
7. Stick to the things you know you can do well
8. Challenge yourself continually about business performance and values
9. Tell it like it is – honesty about good and bad performance pays off
10. Beware of allowing success to lead to complacency

10 WAYS TO WIN BUSINESS

1. Know the pond you are paddling in, i.e. understand the marketplace
2. Have supreme confidence in the quality of your goods and services
3. Have supreme confidence in the team around you
4. Spend your marketing money wisely
5. Meet your customers' deadlines
6. Exceed your customers' expectations
7. Enjoy frequent compliments/complaints sessions with your customers
8. Consider all feedback and act upon it
9. Reward customer loyalty
10. Maintain high morale amongst the customer service deliverers

10 WAYS TO IMPROVE RETAIL SALES

1. Work hard to have the right service people on the right shifts always
2. Strive to have the best product availability, range and choice available always
3. Train and train again to ensure customer service is consistently high standard
4. Measure training and delivery by monitoring customer delight via feedback
5. Be very clear about your points of difference and competitive advantages
6. Devote time to planning sales promotions and unbeatable offers that will attract sales
7. See the process of pre-sale, sale and after sales service as a complete cycle
8. Consider product demonstrations to help customers' decision to buy
9. Consider leaflets and information sheets as a useful digest to the best offers available
10. Assess, assess and assess again your offer and service – and keep driving improvements

10 THOUGHTS ON SALES PROMOTION

1. Create in-store displays with maximum impact in prime locations
2. Erect special fixtures and display stands to attract interest
3. Use strong signage (banners, posters, etc.) to draw attention and shout the offers
4. Highlight buy one-get-one free, three-for-two, multi-save, multi-buy promotions
5. Consider distinctive packaging or on-pack stickers to highlight offers
6. Design leaflets, catalogues, tip sheets, etc., to educate and inform
7. Install audio-visual support to illustrate and entertain
8. Organise special event evenings and competitions
9. Plan for exciting demonstration and sampling areas
10. Advertise as much as you can afford

4. LESSONS ABOUT GETTING THE BEST OUT OF INDIVIDUALS AND TEAMS

10 WAYS TO GET THINGS DONE

1. Decide if action needs to be taken at all
2. Once made, don't wrestle with the decision, just get on with it
3. Always remember, getting things done is what you are paid to do
4. Better start today than tomorrow, if practical
5. Aim to complete the task to the best of your ability, heart and soul
6. Whatever you decide, remember it is your decision, so own it completely
7. Enjoy the process and learn from the journey
8. Give yourself a secret personal incentive and strive for it
9. Think of the benefits to the business, the team and yourself
10. Involve the whole team, lead but delegate

10 LESSONS ABOUT LISTENING

1. Fix your concentration completely on the person speaking
2. Listen calmly and professionally
3. Listen as they talk but leave your analysis and judgement until later
4. Learn to take notes in your head
5. Keep your body language open and welcoming
6. Avoid closed questions when probing for more understanding
7. Allow the speaker plenty of time to finish what they are saying
8. Interrupt only if you have something relevant to say
9. Guide them towards the crux of the matter
10. Be prepared for mixed emotions

10 WAYS TO NURTURE TEAM INVOLVEMENT

1. Lead by example
2. Involve, involve, involve everybody in everything
3. Be available for anyone, anytime
4. Give individuals wide but clear parameters to do more than their job
5. Praise successes however minor
6. Coach people out of failures by identifying opportunities
7. Encourage fun, laughter and team socialising
8. Talk to each member of your direct team at least once a day
9. Keep everyone informed about the state of the business, warts and all
10. Encourage ambitions to do well

10 TIME MANAGEMENT TIPS

1. Start by saying: "It's my life, therefore my time, so I'm in charge of it"
2. See your diary as an opportunity to organise rather than a millstone
3. Plan each week one week ahead, including time for you
4. Allocate specific time periods for meetings and stick to them
5. Use different coloured pens to distinguish priorities etc from the rest
6. Wherever you work, keep the place tidy
7. The more you say "Yes", the more your time will be wasted – learn to say "No"
8. Delegate as much as you can, without losing your grip on the important things
9. Become more decisive, decisions in seconds rather than hours or days
10. Use a kitchen-timer on your desk to help discipline your day's work

10 WAYS TO GET FEEDBACK IF YOU REALLY WANT SOME

1. There is no simpler way to get feedback than to ask for it
2. Ask for it from people who will tell you the truth
3. Listen carefully to everything that is being said
4. Absorb the feedback in a relaxed state of mind
5. Listen to it or read it from the perspective of a third person
6. Take time to process the feedback slowly and carefully
7. Clarify anything, but do it rationally, not as a cross-examination
8. Reflect on it, enjoy the compliments and start acting upon the criticisms
9. Devise a personal development plan to improve whatever needs work
10. Thank the feedbackers because they might just have done you a favour

10 THINGS TO STOP YOU WORRYING

1. Take control of the concern and work on the things you can change
2. Manage outcomes and expectations to avoid piling on more worries
3. Take time to get to the heart of the issue that's bugging you
4. Accentuate the positive, as the song goes and eliminate the negative
5. Stay calm, don't panic because a solution is out there
6. Write down the things you are worrying about and the actions to resolve
7. Don't be afraid to change tactics when looking for a way through
8. Talk to family, friends and colleagues – they just might have the answer
9. Book time for yourself in the park, at the cinema, in a coffee shop, etc
10. Remember every problem has a solution

10 ALARM BELLS SUGGESTING YOU ARE UNHAPPY AT WORK

1. You get isolated, cold-shouldered and sense communication blackout
2. You feel that expressing an opinion is becoming a real effort
3. Your heart sinks when you see or are in your workplace
4. Your yawn-rate has increased during working hours
5. You spend more time than you should mentally assassinating colleagues
6. You have taken all your holiday entitlement by mid-April
7. You spend Sundays dreading Mondays
8. You take every last second of your lunch break
9. You resent putting money into colleagues' birthday or leaving gifts
10. Your eyes glaze over when you see your company's TV advertisements

10 THINGS TO PONDER WHEN IN A PREDICAMENT

1. Identify the issue clearly by thinking it through, then writing it down
2. Whatever it is, do a SWOT (strengths, weaknesses, opportunities, threats)
3. Dwell on your strengths and believe that you can overcome the problem
4. Talk it through with someone you trust enough to let fly if necessary
5. Take time to go for a walk in the fresh air to settle your thoughts
6. Do not allow the worrying to get into the driving seat
7. Consider short, medium and long-term solutions
8. Decide on the whole strategic solution or at least one small step
9. When you are ready, make your decision and get on with implementing it
10. Give yourself a mental round of applause

5. LESSONS FROM THE WORLD AROUND US

10 BUSINESS-RELATED QUOTATIONS

1. "If you are going through hell, keep going."

    Winston Churchill

2. "A memorandum is written not to inform the reader but to protect the writer."

    Dean Acheson

3. "A leader is a dealer in hope."

    Napoleon Bonaparte

4. "Pennies do not come from heaven, they have to be earned here on earth."

    Margaret Thatcher

5. "If you have a job without aggravations, you don't have a job."

    Malcolm Forbes

6. "You're only as good as the people you hire."

    Ray Kroc

7. "Sometimes words can serve me well and sometimes words can go to hell."

    Harry Chapin

8. "All animals, except man, know that the principal business of life is to enjoy it."

    Samuel Butler

9. "As long as you're thinking anyway, think big."

    Donald Trump

10. "You can't get from here to there without taking risks. You win some, you lose some."

    Sir Philip Green

10 BEATLES SONGS TO PROMPT YOU INTO ACTION

1. *We Can Work It Out* – every problem has a solution
2. *A Hard Day's Night* – no-one told you work was going to be easy
3. *I Should Have Known Better* – the learning curve never straightens out
4. *Help!* – if you need it, don't be too proud to ask
5. *Ob-La-Di-Ob-La-Da* – because sometimes it's good to be a little silly
6. *The Long And Winding Road* – every career and project is a journey
7. *Eight Days A Week* – ditch the 24/7 trend; balance your life's priorities
8. *Let It Be* – sometimes you've got to back off or move on
9. *Revolution* – occasionally necessary but most businesses prefer evolution
10. *Taxman* – because there's always a bogeyman to keep us on our toes

10 BOB DYLAN SONGS TO MAKE YOU THINK

1. *A Hard Rain's A-Gonna Fall* – bad things happen, expect it and deal with it
2. *The Times They Are A-Changin'* – business is an ever-moving beast
3. *It Takes A Lot To Laugh, It Takes A Train To Cry* – stay human
4. *Desolation Row* – work and success are incentives not to go there
5. *One Of Us Must Know* – somebody in the team has an answer or an idea
6. *I Forgot More Than You'll Ever Know* – be experienced but not cocky
7. *Forever Young* – stay fresh and interested, rejecting old sage grumpiness
8. *Gonna Change My Way Of Thinking* – stay flexible, it's a team game
9. *One More Cup Of Coffee* – take five, it's part of the day's work
10. *Subterranean Homesick Blues* – just because it rocks like a monkey!

10 ROLLING STONES SONGS FOR JOB SATISFACTION

1. *Come On* – play your part in getting the business motivated
2. *Start Me Up* – see above
3. *19th Nervous Breakdown* – remember that work/life balance thing?
4. *You Can't Always Get What You Want* – but you can try
5. *Tumbling Dice* – take some calculated risks occasionally
6. *Mixed Emotions* – work can be a soap opera, so treat it accordingly
7. *Rock And A Hard Place* – dilemmas are part of the mix
8. *You Don't Have To Mean It* – oh yes you do!
9. *Time Is On My Side* – do you really think so? Use it wisely.
10. *Jumpin' Jack Flash* – because sometimes a little air guitar energises you

10 COMMANDMENTS ADAPTED FOR BUSINESS

1. First – I am the Boss, your Guv'ner – 'nuff said
2. Second – you shall not take the name of the Boss, your Guv'ner, in vain
3. Third – remember to work your socks off every day
4. Fourth – respect your parents as you'll need them to babysit when you do overtime
5. Fifth – you shall not kill, unless provoked by a really irritating person (joke!)
6. Sixth – you shall not steal, 'cos you will be cuffed and your job will be stuffed
7. Seventh – you shall not have work relationships, office party or not
8. Eighth – you shall not lie and stitch up your career rivals
9. Ninth – you shall not run off with the Boss's partner
10. Tenth – you shall not be allowed to have ideas above your station

10 PROVERBS OFFERING GOOD OLD-FASHIONED WISDOM

1. A bad workman always blames his tools
2. A chain is only as strong as its weakest link
3. Actions speak louder than words
4. Bad news travels fast
5. Civility costs nothing
6. Don't cut off your nose to spite your face
7. Don't put all your eggs in one basket
8. Experience is the best teacher
9. Honesty is the best policy
10. Patience is a virtue

10 MOTTOES TO INSPIRE

1. Be Prepared *(Scout Association)*
2. Watch Well (Gardez Bien) *(Montgomery Clan)*
3. My Word Is My Bond (Dictum Meum Pactum) *(Stock Exchange)*
4. I Serve (Ich Dien) *(Prince of Wales)*
5. Justice Is The Queen Of the Virtues (Justita Virtutum Regina) *(Goldsmiths Company)*
6. Nation Shall Speak Peace Unto Nation *(BBC)*
7. Through Endeavour To The Stars (Per Ardua Ad Astra) *(RAF)*
8. By Reason And Counsel (Ratione Et Concilio) *(Magistrates Association)*
9. Always Faithful (Semper Fidelis) *(Devonshire Regiment)*
10. Who Dares Wins *(SAS)*

A GUIDE TO HELP YOU DIG DEEP AND THINK LONG AND HARD

THINGS TO CONSIDER	UNDERSTAND WHAT GOES ON	DIG DEEPER	THINK WIDER	THINK IT OVER AGAIN
WHAT?	What is our business and what are we doing with it?	What are the benefits of doing business our way?	What else could we do to change and/or improve things?	What should we be doing differently, if anything?
WHEN?	When are we open for business?	Are we open when customers want us?	Are we fully accessible and convenient?	When else could we increase sales?
WHERE?	Where do we do business?	Is the location and building right?	Does we match the catchment area's needs?	Where else could we do business?
HOW?	How do we conduct ourselves?	How do or customers feel about us?	How could we improve our image?	How much do we need to change?
WHO?	Who is on our team?	Is everyone working well?	Do we need to change anyone?	Who would improve the team?

HOW TO GET IDEAS FOR BUSINESS IMPROVEMENT FROM YOUR TEAM

Employee involvement in business improvement is important. The table below should be given to each employee, regardless of job role, to stimulate a collection of practical ideas. Sometimes, a little incentive for the best ideas can help oil the cogs. Asking the team to complete this exercise every three months will maintain momentum.

FOCUS AREAS	WHAT'S THE IDEA?	WHAT'S THE BENEFIT?	IS IT EASILY DONE?	WHAT'S THE COST?	WHAT'S THE FIRST STEP?
IMPROVE THE SHOP					
IMPROVE CUSTOMER SERVICE					
IMPROVE TEAM MORALE					
IMPROVE THE BUSINESS GENERALLY					

If you have any comments on this book or ideas for future writing projects, or if you would like to discuss ways in which I can help your business and team with practical advice and support, please contact me on joecushnan@aol.com.

Areas of experience and expertise:
- Retail operations
- Individual and team training, development, coaching and mentoring
- General business improvements
- Question & answer sessions to share knowledge and stories
- Career advice